In Memory

Kathleen "Nanny" McPhillips
The best grandmother a boy could ever hope to have.

Dedicated to…

Jim and Mary McPhillips, my parents, the first to teach me that our
Catholic Faith is such a precious gift.

Nihil Obstat: Father Mark S. Ott, MDiv, MA, SSL Censor
                 Deputatus

Imprimatur: Most Reverend Richard G. Lennon, MTh, MA Bishop
                 of Cleveland

                 Given at Cleveland, Ohio, on 19 December 2016.

                 The Nihil Obstat and Imprimatur are official
                 declarations that a book or pamphlet is free of doctrinal
                 or moral error. No implication is contained therein that
                 those who have granted the Nihil Obstat and Imprimatur
                 agree with the contents, opinion, or statements
                 expressed.

1

Table of Contents

Preface

As I look at my life I realize how good the Lord has been to me. I have parents who love me and made so many sacrifices for me and my siblings. I had a grandmother whose love of the Lord and His Blessed Mother deeply touched my heart. I had seminary professors and classmates whose guidance and friendship helped keep me firmly rooted in our Catholic Faith. I have been so richly blessed!

This book has been a long time coming. It is the result of so many people who inspired me to seek our Lord and allow Him to more and more rule my heart. And while I still have a long way to go in the spiritual life, I have great hopes that these reflections will help others come to a deeper love of our Lord and His Blessed Mother.

I do need to thank Dr. Anthony Iezzi who was my mentor in college and was so instrumental in my formation in our Catholic Faith. My Uncle Tom, whose devotion to the faith touched me at the core of my being. Karl Keating, the founder of Catholic Answers, in his book *Catholicism and Fundamentalism* first inspired my love of apologetics. Franciscan University in Steubenville with their "Defending the Faith" conferences has given me so many insights that inspire me to a greater love of the Divine Mysteries reflected upon in this book.

A special mention needs to be made of Dr. Scott Hahn whose CD's and books have had a huge impact on my life and priesthood. As a convert to the faith Dr. Hahn has a love of scripture and our Catholic Faith that makes both really "come alive" in his speaking and writing. I could probably footnote him on every other page of this book, so much have I "borrowed" from him in my own preaching and writing. I would certainly encourage you to turn to Dr. Hahn's talks and books to help you come to a deeper understanding of the bible and our faith.

Much of this book took shape at the South Caroline home of Joe and Becky Williams. Their kindness and support to me has been a great blessing in my life and very much contributed to this book finally coming to fruition.

Finally, a very special thank you to Marilyn Bottger, who edited this book for me, Vicky Fedor, who suggested the title, Mary Weber and Linda Koeth who read and offered suggestions, Shari Jamieson who provided the art work, and Jim Hogan who did so much in formatting the book. May God bless them all!

Fr. Jay McPhillips
Pastor: St. Helen Church, Newbury, Ohio

Introduction

I was born in the late 1950s and came of age in the 60s and 70s. It was a time of rapid change and tumult in our country and great confusion in the Church. Pope John XXIII called Vatican II "to open the windows of the Church," but there can be no doubt that those open windows allowed gale force winds into the Church causing great confusion.

When I was growing up many of the traditional devotions were being pushed aside and even the ones that were practiced seemed more perfunctory then genuine expressions of love for God and His plan. For instance, I participated in "May Crownings" in the classroom, but it never imparted to me a deep love and reverence for the Blessed Mother.

As I grew Mary was never a big part of my spiritual life. Even when I was in high school and had what some might call a "born again" experience, the Blessed Mother just was not a part of it. While I came to a deep love of Jesus and a dedication to His Church, Mary was very much on the periphery. In the seminary I viewed Mary more as an "ecumenical problem" then as someone who was essential to the faith.

That indifference toward Mary was even continued into my priesthood. If someone asked me to lead a rosary at a wake I would find myself filled with anxiety because I really did not know how to pray the rosary correctly, it just was not a part of my spiritual life. While I believed in the teaching of the Church about the Immaculate Conception and the Assumption, I often felt it was much ado about nothing. Who cared? I felt I could practice my faith without giving much thought to Mary.

My attitude changed drastically in the summer of 1988. I had just been reassigned to St. Helen Church in Newbury, Ohio. I received word of a tragic accident involving a teenage boy from the parish. His name was Alan Bates and he had been working with his father early on a Monday morning. They had gone to a supply house to get some materials for the job they had to do. The father, Al Sr, told his son to load some pipe on the truck and he would go inside to pay for it. There were palates of pipe all stacked on top of each other. Alan took some wire cutters and cut the straps on one of the middle palates. The pipes of that palate fell out and the palates above it all shifted; they fell on Alan crushing him. He was rushed to the hospital in a coma.

I had the privilege of visiting Alan and his family several times in the next month before Alan died. Every time I came, his mother Joyce was at his bedside. Often, she would be holding his hand whispering to him how much she loved him, begging him to recover. There was no doubt in my mind that she would do anything to trade places with the son she loved so much!

On one of my trips home, it was as if Jesus slapped me on the side of my head saying, "Do you get it now? Do you understand now a mother's love? Do you understand how My Mother shared in my passion and death? Do you understand that no one in the history of the world suffered with Me as My mother?" My attitude toward Mary and my prayer life changed on that day. While I still pondered the role of Mary in salvation and my own spiritual life, I was never again dismissive of Mary's role.

Sharing in the Suffering of Jesus

One aspect of the Christian faith often missed by our separated brothers and sisters is the role of our suffering in God's plan of salvation. St. Paul teaches us in Rom 8:14-17:

> *For those who are led by the Spirit of God are children of God. For you did not receive a spirit of slavery to fall back into fear, but you received a spirit of adoption, through which we cry, "Abba, Father!" The Spirit itself bears witness with our spirit that we are children of God, and if children, then heirs, heirs of God and joint heirs with Christ, if only we suffer with him so that we may also be glorified with him.*

The part about being children of God and heirs of God and joint heirs with Christ is so beautiful and hopeful, but why did he have to bring up that suffering part? That does not sound very hopeful! It is as if St. Paul anticipated my objections because he goes on to say in Rom 8:18-23:

> *I consider that the sufferings of this present time are as nothing compared with the glory to be revealed for us. For creation awaits with eager expectation the revelation of the children of God; for creation was made subject to futility, not of its own accord but because of the one who subjected it, in hope that creation itself would be set free from slavery to corruption and share in the glorious freedom of the children of God. We know that all creation is groaning in labor pains even until now; and not only that, but we ourselves, who have the first fruits of the Spirit, we also groan within ourselves as we wait for adoption, the redemption of our bodies.*

7

St. Paul is saying that we have to suffer here, but it is nothing compared to the glory God has in store for us. That all creation is groaning right now, and we groan in a world filled with suffering. But why? Why do we have to suffer? If God loves us why does He not remove suffering from our lives and our world? After all, Jesus suffered to save us, our suffering seems pointless! But the Bible tells us a different story. St. Paul says something in the letter to the Colossians that you would think was heresy, if you did not find it in scripture. He tells us in Colossians 1:24, *"Now I rejoice in my sufferings for your sake, and in my flesh, I am filling up what is lacking in the afflictions of Christ on behalf of his body, which is the church..."* How could anything be lacking in the suffering of Christ? And why would anyone rejoice in suffering? In my life I have always viewed suffering as something to be avoided at all cost. Why would anyone rejoice in suffering?

This opens up an incredible insight into the plan of God. We are saved by the suffering of Jesus, but Jesus is not through suffering! He suffers through His Body. That is, He suffers through you and through me! And His suffering through His Body is an essential element in the work of salvation. Jesus has elevated you and me to be co-workers with Him in saving the world. Our suffering is not pointless, it is a sharing in the saving work of the Lord. That is why Jesus tells us that unless we pick up our cross and follow Him we are not worthy of Him (Mt 10:38); that is why St. Peter tells us to rejoice to the extent we share in the sufferings of Jesus (1Peter 4:13). In fact, as you read through 1 Peter you cannot help but notice that Peter sees suffering as a central aspect of living the faith in that he mentions suffering 19 times!

In all honesty when I reflect on the faith, I love to think of God's love for me and the great lengths that Jesus was willing to go for me to be saved. But contemplating that God is calling me to suffer with Jesus was not really on my radar screen early in life. Oh sure, once in a while my mom or one of the nuns would say, "offer it up" when something bad happened, but it never really registered in my brain as something that was important for salvation. But now, when I see the extent of suffering in the world I am forced to contemplate that plan of God. I need to constantly remind myself that God's plan is a plan of love even though I have a hard time seeing the love amid so much suffering. But St. Paul reminds us that God can use our suffering for our salvation and the salvation of others. He assures us that the Spirit will come to the aid of our weakness (Rom 8:26) and that God will make all things work out right in the end for those who love Him (Rom 8:28). He goes on to tell us that suffering does not separate us from Christ, but draws us closer to Him. In that beautiful passage from Rom 8:35-39 that is so often misunderstood St. Paul tells us:

> *What will separate us from the love of Christ? Will anguish, or distress, or persecution, or famine, or nakedness, or peril, or the sword? As it is written: 'For your sake we are being slain all the day; we are looked upon as sheep to be slaughtered.'*

> *No, in all these things we conquer overwhelmingly through him who loved us. For I am convinced that neither death, nor life, nor angels, nor principalities, nor present things, nor future things, nor powers, nor height, nor depth, nor any other creature will be able to separate us from the love of God in Christ Jesus our Lord.*

Some interpret this to mean that once we are saved that we have an assurance of salvation no matter what we might do in the future. But notice what St. Paul does not say. He does not ask, "What will separate us from the love of Christ? Will adultery or murder or fornication or abortion or homosexual relations? No, we conquer overwhelmingly through Him." That is not what he says. He asks, "What will separate us from Christ? Will anguish, or distress, or persecution, or famine, or nakedness, or peril, or the sword?" Folks, those are all forms of suffering! Paul is not saying that sin will not separate us from Christ, but that suffering will not. In fact, in suffering we are conformed to Christ (Rom 8:29).

Mary and Suffering

If our suffering is an essential aspect of faith; if our suffering is a part of the work of salvation; if in suffering, we are conformed to Christ and share in His saving work; if the suffering of Christ through His Body leads to salvation for others; then Mary's suffering with her Son has led others to receive the grace of salvation. As we already have seen, no one suffered with Jesus the way His Mother did! It was prophesized by Simeon in Luke 2:35-36:

> ...and Simeon blessed them and said to Mary his mother, "Behold, this child is destined for the fall and rise of many in Israel, and to be a sign that will be contradicted and you yourself a sword will pierce so that the thoughts of many hearts may be revealed."

Mary was to suffer, but it was for a reason. We are to suffer, but there is a reason. We might not fully understand in this life the necessity of suffering, but there is a reason and we need to trust as Mary did, that God will make all things work out right for those who love Him (Rom 8:28).

Mary, Faith and the Rosary

Many people today have had the experience on a renewal or retreat of hearing people share a personal witness to how God has been active in their lives. Often people share of how they were on the wrong path and God brought them back to Him. Other times they speak of tragedy or loss and how God got them through. Most people find these personal witnesses a powerful tool in growing closer to the Lord.

I find it helpful to view the rosary as Mary's personal witness. It is like our Mother is taking us by the hand and saying, "Let me tell you about what my Son has done for me. Let me show you what my Son has done for you." Mary's greatest desire is to help you and me to know and love her Son more fully so that we can serve Him with all our hearts. In my experience as we reflect with Mary on these mysteries of the faith, she not only brings them to our attention, but she helps us to ponder them anew in such a way that they become more and more a part of our lives. Through her intersession we grow in our understanding of the faith so that we can grow in our love of the Lord. In sharing with us the twenty mysteries of faith that we find in the rosary she opens to us a treasure trove of insights into the Bible, her Son and the Christian faith. I know I have found this to be true in my life.

Understanding the Bible

One of the biggest obstacles to understand the plan of God and how the saving work of Jesus is to play out in the world and in our personal lives is when we do not understand the Bible. The Bible is the soul of theology, prayer, and growing closer to the Lord. Unfortunately, many people do not understand how to read the Bible. Of special concern is that many fail to recognize how the Bible is to be read as a coherent unity. The fact is that the whole Bible is about Jesus. The Law and the prophets were all preparing the world for the coming of the Savior.

Unfortunately, many people today fail to see the connections between the Old Testament (OT) and the New Testament (NT). Many see the Bible as analogous to an old NASA rocket. I remember watching space launches as a child. When the rocket got to a certain height part of the rocket would break off and the top would continue. The part that had separated on the bottom had done its work and was no longer necessary for the rest of the mission. That, unfortunately, is how some people view the OT. Except for a few prophesies about the coming of Jesus, they see it as irrelevant to the faith. This leads to a real lack of understanding of the true plan of God.

In the story of Jesus appearing to the disciples on the road to Emmaus on the day of the Resurrection, we are told how the disciples' hearts were burning inside them as Jesus explained the scripture to them (Luke 24:13-35). Interestingly, Luke does not tell us exactly what He said. But it is clear that Jesus shared with them a way of looking at the OT that they had not previously known. And while He would have highlighted several prophetic passages like Isaiah 7:14 that speaks of a virgin conceiving, and the suffering servant passages in Isaiah, and how Psalm 22 was speaking of His saving work. There was much more.

Biblical Types

The biblical writers give us a glimpse of the concept of typology, but they do not explain it in depth. That is probably because all the earliest Christians had been schooled in the methodology and there was no need to explain it when writing the NT. Some of the most fundamental aspects of the faith are often presumed to be known to the readers by the authors of scripture. For instance, the author of Hebrews tells us in 5:11-6:3

> *About this we have much to say, and it is difficult to explain, for you have become sluggish in hearing. Although you should be teachers by this time, you need to have someone teach you again the basic elements of the utterances of God. You need milk, [and] not solid food. Everyone who lives on milk lacks experience of the word of righteousness, for he is a child. But solid food is for the mature, for those whose faculties are trained by practice to discern good and evil.*
>
> *Therefore, let us leave behind the basic teaching about Christ and advance to maturity, without laying the foundation all over again: repentance from dead works and faith in God, instruction about baptisms and laying on of hands, resurrection of the dead and eternal judgment. And we shall do this, if only God permits.*

The writer of Hebrews chastises them for not understanding the basics and saying that he is not going to explain the rudimentary elements of the faith. Unfortunately, many today read the Bible without knowing the basic elements of the faith and very much distort the message of the scriptures.

One of the most basic principles of the scriptures is the principle of biblical types. A type is a person, place or thing in the OT that was meant to prefigure a person, place or thing in the NT. Understanding the type helps us to understand the fulfillment of the type in the NT. Without understanding the OT type we will most likely not understand the fulfillment in the NT.

So, for instance in Rom 5:14 St. Paul casually mentions that Adam was a type of Christ, but he does not feel any need to explain what that means. Why not? He expected that all of his readers who had been trained in the faith would immediately understand the meaning. But today many do not understand typology so that teaching of Paul goes by us unnoticed. Knowing that Adam was a type of Christ gives us insight into the Church and how she was formed. How is that? Well when we look at Genesis we see that Adam was put into a deep sleep and from his side the bride of Adam was formed. This helps us understand the excitement of St. John when he tells us in his gospel chapter 19:31-35:

> *Now since it was preparation day, in order that the bodies might not remain on the cross on the Sabbath, for the Sabbath day of that week was a solemn one, the Jews asked Pilate that their legs be broken and they be taken down. So the soldiers came and broke the legs of the first and then of the other one who was crucified with Jesus. But when they came to Jesus and saw that he was already dead, they did not break his legs, but one soldier thrust his lance into his side, and immediately blood and water flowed out. An eyewitness has testified, and his testimony is true; he knows that he is speaking the truth, so that you also may [come to] believe.*

Why did St. John get so excited in verse 35? It was because he knew that Adam was a type of Christ. When Jesus, the new Adam, is in the sleep of death on the cross His side is opened and out comes water (symbolizing baptism) and blood (symbolizing the Holy Eucharist); these are the two primary sacraments that form the Bride of Christ, the Church. If we do not know typology this imagery would be totally lost on us.

14

There are many types of Christ. Melchizadek, Isaac, Moses, Aaron, the Passover Lamb, David, Solomon, Jonah, the seraph serpent mounted on the pole, the temple, etc.

As we go through the Bible we see that there are types of baptism [the creation of the world, the great flood, and the Israelites passing through the Red Sea]. There are types of the Holy Eucharist [the Manna in the desert; the Bread of the Presence that was kept in the holy of holies along with a carafe of wine; the sacrifice of the first priest, Melchizadek when he offered bread and wine in Gen 14:18-20; the "Todah" (thanksgiving) sacrifices that involved offering bread and wine to God.]

And there were types of Mary [Eve; the Ark of the Covenant; Bethsheba and the other Queen Mothers of ancient Judah; Noah's Ark; Jacob's ladder; the burning bush; Sarah, the wife of Abraham; Rebecca, the wife of Isaac; Rachel, the beautiful wife of Jacob; Miriam, the sister of Moses; Deborah the prophetess; Judith; Esther; etc. (For an explanation of each of these types please see *Introduction to Mary* by Mark Miraville)]. In this book we will focus primarily on Eve, The Ark of the Covenant, and the Queen Mothers of Judah as pointing us to Mary.

One of the most essential principles to understand as we speak of types is the fact that the NT fulfillment of a type is always far greater than the original type. St. Paul points out this principle in 2 Cor 3:9-11 when he states:

> *For if the ministry of condemnation was glorious, the ministry of righteousness will abound much more in glory. Indeed, what was endowed with glory has come to have no glory in this respect because of the glory that surpasses it. For if what was*

going to fade was glorious, how much more will what endures be glorious.

Paul says that compared to the glory of the NT any glory in the OT must be considered "no glory." This principle gives us incredible insight into the meaning of the NT. For instance, we pointed out above that the great flood was a type of baptism. By this principle whenever a person is baptized that is a greater event then the great flood. How could that be? We are speaking of almost all life being wiped away in the flood; how could that be less of an event than someone being baptized? It is because the great flood dealt only with the physical world, in baptism the life of God is infused into a human soul. God is greater than all of creation, so the infusing of God's life into a soul is a greater event than the flood in Noah's day. The glory of the NT far surpasses that of the OT.

This helps us see why so many of our separated brothers and sisters do not understand the Bible or the sacraments. After all, if baptism is only a symbol, then it is nowhere nearly as glorious as the great flood. In fact, as a fulfillment of a type, you would have to conclude that the events of the OT were far greater than their fulfillment. That, of course, would make a lie of St. Paul's teaching in 2 Cor 3.

The same is true when you look at the Holy Eucharist being the fulfillment of the OT type of manna in the desert. Think of what occurred during the Israelites' sojourn in the desert; tens of thousands of people were miraculously fed for 40 years with "bread from heaven." If the Holy Eucharist is only a symbol, as many of our separated brothers and sisters claim, you would need to conclude that the OT types were far greater than their fulfillment. That again would make a lie of St. Paul's teaching in 2 Corinthians 3. But the truth is that the Holy Eucharist is not just a symbol; the Holy Eucharist is the actual body, blood, soul and divinity of Jesus present in our midst. It is God coming to His people. When we recognize the truth of the Holy Eucharist, we see that the fulfillment is far greater than the type, since the manna was only physical bread while the Eucharist is God Himself. Again, the glory of the NT far surpasses that of the OT.

We will examine throughout this book how Mary is the fulfillment of OT types. We will see the glory of the original Ark of the Covenant and that will lead us to see how even more glorious Mary is. We will see the incredible respect paid to the Queen Mothers of ancient Judah. How much greater respect is due to the Mother of God!

Why the Rosary?

The rosary as we will see is a beautiful way to reflect on the Bible and the great mysteries of faith. Our Mother Mary takes us by the hand and helps us to contemplate all her Son has done for each of us as individuals and what He has done for the world.

It is also an invaluable tool in obeying Jesus' command that we pray for our enemies and others who have hurt us in life (Mt 5:44). In the past when I would pray for people I was angry at or who had hurt me in any way, my prayer would be something like this: "God, give him the grace to realize what an idiot he is! Open her eyes to see how much she has hurt other people. Make him aware of what a creep he really is." When I would "pray for people" in this manner, I only found myself angrier about the person than I had been before I prayed for them. I now pray the rosary or a decade of the rosary for people who have hurt me. In praying this way my focus is not on the person's faults and failings (as I see them), but rather my focus is on the great things God in His mercy has done for me and the world. I pray for the

17

person I'm angry at or hurt by; but my focus is on God not the faults of the other.

I personally have found this a great gift in praying for others. It has certainly been much more spiritually beneficial than focusing on the failings of the people around me. I certainly encourage husbands and wives to pray for one another with Mary. It is a wonderful way for parents to pray for children; teachers to pray for their students, brothers and sisters to pray for one another; bishops to pray for their priests; and priests, their Bishop.

It is also very helpful for citizens to pray for their political leaders with Mary's aid. I know when I have prayed for the Supreme Court, or the president or certain members of congress in the past; I did not finish the prayer with feelings of great love for them. In praying with Mary, I have made progress in that area, although in honesty I still have a long way to go. But with Mary's aid my prayers no longer end with feelings of great disgust as was often the case in the past. The rosary is so helpful in helping us realize how much we are in need of the mercy of God and can help us to think of others in terms of mercy as well.

The Method for this Book

Pope John Paul the Great in his Apostolic Letter *Rosarium Virginis Mariae (The Rosary of the Virgin Mary),* added the Luminous Mysteries of the rosary. At the time he offered suggestions on praying the rosary with greater spiritual benefit. He suggested that in the prayer "Hail Mary" that the name of Jesus was at the center. He said it would be helpful to add a reflection at that point as a way of aiding the one who prays to keep focus on the mystery. That suggestion very much changed my prayer life which led to this book. In these pages you will find a reflection for each of the 203 Hail Marys prayed in the entire rosary (all four sets of mysteries).

I refer to some of these reflections as **"primary reflections;"** designated by the initial **(P).** Often the first of the ten reflections and the last will be a similar reflection, but not always. These primary reflections could be used for the entire mystery because it is usually what I see as the overall, or at least a central theme for the mystery. These primary reflections often give insight into understanding the Bible or some important tenet of the faith.

It is important to remember however, that these reflections did not come down from on high. They are not given to us by God Himself. These reflections are one sinful man's insights. You may see some of the other reflections as being more beneficial than the ones I have designated as primary. You might want to insert reflections other than the ones you find in the following pages. Please adapt this in any way that you find personally helpful to you.

Me and Us

As you go through this you will notice that in some of the reflections the words "my" or "me" are used and in other places the words "our" or "us" are employed. Usually at the beginning of the mystery I focus on how Jesus did a particular act for my salvation and at the end I focus on how we are all in this together. For instance, in the 4th Sorrowful Mystery the first reflection is **"who carried the cross for my salvation"** while the last is, **"who carried the cross for the salvation of the world."** In the 2nd Glorious Mystery the first reflection is, **"who ascended into heaven to prepare a place for me;"** while the last is, **"who ascended into heaven to prepare a place for all His faithful people."** I find it helpful to see Jesus' saving work as being done personally for me, however it is also essential to see that He wants us to be a part of the community of faith.

Apologetics and Karate Kid Theology

In the classic movie *The Karate Kid* we are told the story of a boy named Daniel who is being bullied. An elderly gardener (Miyagi) agrees to teach him karate, but it appears that Miyagi is more interested in having Daniel work on his deck and wax cars than teaching him karate. At one-point Daniel yells at Miyagi about how he is wasting his time, but then Miyagi attempts to strike Daniel who uses the same motion he had been using in waxing cars to deflect Miyagi's punch. Miyagi throws another punch and Daniel again uses the same motion to block the punch. The teacher explains that the repetition of waxing cars and scrubbing decks is preparing him to block the punches of others. It's a great scene!

Many Catholics today find themselves under attack from their Evangelical and Fundamentalist friends, co-workers, and family members. They often find themselves at a loss to explain the Catholic faith and why we believe what we do.

This book is written from an apologetics point of view. Apologetics is not referring to apologizing for the faith, but rather how to defend the faith. Many of the reflections involve the issues on which many of our separated brothers and sisters disagree with us. Praying the mysteries of the rosary repeatedly, coupled with what you learn in this book, will equip you to have answers when you are challenged on the faith.

We of course always want to respond to our brothers and sisters with charity. We are not out to win arguments, but to share the truth of our

Catholic faith. With Mary's help you can delve more fully into the depths of our faith and share those saving truths with others.

At the end of the original *Karate Kid* movie, Daniel was able to stand up against others and defend himself. The movements Miyagi taught him gave Daniel the confidence to live his life to the fullest. It is my hope that in reading this book and then reflecting on the mysteries of the rosary (which will reinforce and constantly call to mind what you have learned) that you will gain the confidence to be able to explain the Catholic faith and the Bible to others.

Pray Always

Jesus and St. Paul both encourage us to pray always (Lk 18:1 & Eph 6:18). The rosary is a wonderful way to do just that. I often pray the rosary while doing my exercise. In an hour on the treadmill or the exercise bike I can pray all four sets of mysteries. I often pray the rosary while driving, although it takes longer to pray while in the car because of all the distractions on the road. I find that praying the rosary while driving cuts down substantially on road rage. Hopefully you will find the same thing in your life.

In the past when driving I would listen to talk radio and would find myself getting so angry about the state of our world. Now instead of getting angry about the problems of the world, I pray for God's grace on our leaders and people. When taking a walk in the park or doing my exercise I used to allow my mind to daydream. These daydreams were usually focused on me; now I can walk or exercise and be focused on the incredible gifts God has given to me and the world, as Mary helps me ponder the indescribable mercy of God.

It is my hope and prayer that the rosary will become for you what it has for me: a precious gift leading to a deeper love and trust in our Lord. May our loving Mother take you under her wing and help you to love her Son with all your heart, soul, mind and strength.

Preliminary Prayers

We begin the rosary with the sign of the cross followed by the ancient prayer, the Apostles Creed. This prayer contains 12 articles of faith. Legend tells us that each of the twelve Apostles contributed one of the articles and that it was composed on the day of Pentecost. However, there is much debate and questioning of the origin of the actual Creed as it comes to us today. Many would argue that it was not written by the Apostles per se, but is believed to contain a summary of their teachings. Furthermore, it has been said that in the early Church, people were to memorize the Apostles Creed and never write it on paper. If that was true it would explain why we have no first or second century copies of the Creed.

Whatever the actual origin, it is believed that the Apostles Creed is a summary of the beliefs of the Apostles themselves. Even in the earliest times, a person coming into the Church needed to profess his or her faith. The Apostles Creed was well known in the 4th Century. It does not address some of the theological issues that arose later in the history of the Church such as the divinity of Christ or the Holy Spirit, but it includes seeds of the fullness of the faith. The prayer is as follows:

I believe in God, the Father almighty,
Creator of heaven and earth,
and in Jesus Christ, his only Son, our Lord,
who was conceived by the Holy Spirit,
born of the Virgin Mary, suffered under Pontius Pilate,

22

was crucified, died and was buried;
he descended into hell; on the third day he rose again
from the dead; he ascended into heaven,
and is seated at the right hand of God the Father almighty; from there
he will come to judge the living and the dead.
I believe in the Holy Spirit, the holy catholic Church,
the communion of saints, the forgiveness of sins,
the resurrection of the body, and life everlasting. Amen.

It does not suit the purposes of this book to enter into an in-depth study of the teachings of the Creed, but I would like to highlight a few things that people find confusing. First, it speaks of Jesus descending into hell. This should not be thought of as the place of eternal damnation, but rather "sheol." Sheol is the place of the dead that all people went to after death during OT times. The word "sheol" is often translated into English as "hades" (which is a Greek word) or the "netherworld" or the "underworld." In ancient Jewish literature it was believed there was a good part of sheol and a bad part of sheol. Some literature implies a really good part, a kind of good part, a kind of bad part and a really bad part. The Apostles Creed affirms the teaching in 1 Pt 3:18-20:

> *For Christ also suffered for sins once, the righteous for the sake of the unrighteous, that he might lead you to God. Put to death in the flesh, he was brought to life in the spirit. In it he also went to preach to the spirits in prison, who had once been disobedient while God patiently waited in the days of Noah during the building of the ark, in which a few persons, eight in all, were saved through water.*

In the Apostles Creed we simply affirm that those who lived before the coming of Jesus could hear and respond to the gospel and be saved.

Secondly, you will notice that the word "catholic" has a small "c" rather than a capital "C". This is using the word not in a denominational sense, but in the word's original meaning which is "universal."

Following the Creed, we pray the Lord's Prayer:

Our Father who art in Heaven,
hallowed be thy name;
thy kingdom come
thy will be done
on earth as it is in heaven.
Give us this day our daily bread;
and forgive us our trespasses
as we forgive those who trespass against us;
and lead us not into temptation,
but deliver us from evil. Amen

The Lord's Prayer contains seven petitions and is very much at the center of the prayer life of many Catholics. There are numerous reflections on the prayer which you would do well to ponder. I would warn you that it is very easy when praying prayers on a regular basis, we can fall into a merely mechanical recitation of words. We want, in our prayer, to focus on the words that are being said, and allow their richness to fill our thoughts and souls. That is particularly true when praying the Lord's Prayer.

After the Lord's Prayer we move to praying the Hail Mary three times. Below you will see how inserting reflections at the center of the Hail Mary works and this will be the pattern we use throughout the book.

Hail Mary, full of grace, the Lord is with you; blessed are you among women, and blessed is the fruit of your womb, **Jesus***:*

1) Who came that we might have faith.

> *Holy Mary, mother of God, pray for us sinners*
> *now and at the hour of death. Amen*

Hail Mary, full of grace, the Lord is with you; blessed are you among women, and blessed is the fruit of your womb, **Jesus***:*

2) Who came that we might have hope.

> *Holy Mary, mother of God, pray for us sinners*
> *now and at the hour of death. Amen*

Hail Mary, full of grace, the Lord is with you; blessed are you among women, and blessed is the fruit of your womb, **Jesus***:*

3) Who came to teach us how to love.

> *Holy Mary, mother of God, pray for us sinners*
> *now and at the hour of death. Amen*

Throughout the rest of the book, when we list the reflections, we will simply write the first half of the Hail Mary at the beginning of the chapter, followed by the ten reflections. At the end of the chapter we will write the second half of the prayer, but it is meant to be prayed as we demonstrated above.

In the rest of the book what was written above will appear as follows:

*Hail Mary, full of grace, the Lord is with you; blessed are you among women, and blessed is the fruit of your womb, **Jesus**:*

1) **Who came that we might have faith.**
2) **Who came that we might have hope.**
3) **Who came to teach us how to love.**

Holy Mary, mother of God, pray for us sinners now and at the hour of death. Amen

These are the three theological virtues. As St. Paul teaches in Gal 5:6 we are, "saved by faith working in love." Faith is the virtue that allows us to trust God and surrender to His Will. Hope is the virtue that allows us to face the heartaches and pains of our lives with peace and serenity because we know that Jesus will make all things work out right in the end for those who love Him (Rom 8:28).

Love of course is the greatest virtue. The Bible tells us that "God is love" (1 John 4:8). We are made in the image and likeness of God (Genesis 1:27). Which means that we are made to love.

Our culture however does not understand love. Our culture sees love as a warm, fuzzy feeling that we fall into and out of. For our culture, love is something we have no control over. We cannot control our feeling. But God commands us to love. He does not command us to have feelings we cannot control. Love is not a mere feeling, but a choice; a choice to make the needs and wants of the one loved as important as, or more important than our own needs and wants.

Jesus hanging on the cross was not a pretty sight, but the world has never seen greater love. True love requires sacrifice. It requires giving of oneself for the one loved. Love requires giving until it hurts and then giving some more. To love requires a self-emptying.

Look at a parent taking care of his or her child. Getting up in the middle of the night to feed a hungry baby; cleaning up puke from a sick child; working long hours to provide for a child. That sacrifice is at the heart of love. Love is not easy, but we are made to love. Without love life has no meaning. Without love there cannot be a deep and abiding joy. It is one of the great mysteries of life, love is not easy, but it is what gives meaning and joy to our existence.

One of my all-time favorite works of literature is Dickens' *A Christmas Carol*. In that classic story Scrooge has money and power but he is a miserable unhappy old man. Bob Cratchet who works for him is in deep poverty; he has a handicapped child and many more mouths to feed, but his home is filled with joy. Why? Because Bob Cratchet and his family have love. Bob Cratchet finds great joy in carrying his handicapped son on his shoulder. Giving of himself out of love brings him joy. The fact is it is impossible for a selfish person to find real joy. Oh, they may have moments of fleeting happiness as they get their own way, but it is a superficial happiness that does not last. Love brings true joy and great happiness, but it requires a giving of self.

Why? Because we are made in the image and likeness of God who is love. In our understanding the Father has poured Himself out for all eternity in the begetting of the Son. The Son has poured Himself out for all eternity in giving of Himself to the Father; the Holy Spirit is the bond of love between the two. We are made in the image and likeness of the God who constantly pours Himself out in love. Unless we give of ourselves; unless we empty ourselves; unless we sacrifice ourselves for God and others we cannot find joy.

Jesus came to teach us how to love. If you want to understand love, look at the crucifix. If you want true joy, live a life of love.

We live in a world where more and more people have adopted the attitude of "take care of #1." And as a result, we have more and more people who are basically unhappy. We have more and more people turning to drugs (legal and illegal) to escape the emotional pain of their lives. Why? Because selfish people cannot be happy. Only when we freely give of ourselves in love (love always has to be free) can we find joy. The more western civilization pulls away from the wisdom of God, the more misery we will experience. Our common sense sees sacrifice and self- denial as great enemies to happiness, but God's wisdom shows us that only with self-giving love can we find joy. Until we as a culture once again embrace the saving wisdom of God, we will continue in a downward spiral toward ever deepening despair.

As we pray the rosary we can enter more fully into the mysteries of our faith. In doing that we enter more fully into the love of our God. Faith and love go hand in hand. In the rosary, it is as if Our Lady takes us by the hand and says to us, "Let me tell you about what my Son has done for me. Let me tell you what my Son has done for you." Mary knows our God intimately and her greatest desire is to share the wisdom of the Lord with us so that we might come to know and love her Son more fully. So, let us with Mary enter more fully into the saving mysteries of our faith.

Section 1

The

Joyful

Mysteries

The First Joyful Mystery
The Annunciation

*Hail Mary, full of grace, the Lord is with you; blessed are you among women, and blessed is the fruit of your womb, **Jesus**:*

1) Who chose Mary from all eternity to be His Mother. (P)

For God there is no time. The first day of creation, the day Jesus was born, the day Jesus died on the cross, the day you were born, the last day of the world are all one to God. Mary was chosen by God for an essential role in salvation history.

We see throughout the Bible how God insists that sacred objects must be perfect- every detail needs to be as God directs. We see that with the Ark of the Covenant (which was a type of Mary- Exodus 25:10-22); we see it with the tabernacle in the desert (Exodus 26:1-36); we see that with the building of the Temple and we see that with Mary. Let's take a look at what happened when the angel came to Mary in Luke 1:26-38:

> *In the sixth month, the angel Gabriel was sent from God to a town of Galilee called Nazareth, to a virgin betrothed to a man named Joseph, of the house of David, and the virgin's name was Mary. And coming to her, he said, "Hail, favored one! The Lord is with you. But she was greatly troubled at what was said and pondered what sort of greeting this might be. Then the angel said to her, "Do not be afraid, Mary, for you have found favor with God. Behold, you will conceive in your womb and bear a son, and you shall name him Jesus. He will be great and will be called Son of the Most High and the Lord God will give*

him the throne of David his father, and he will rule over the house of Jacob forever, and of his kingdom there will be no end. But Mary said to the angel, "How can this be, since I have no relations with a man?" And the angel said to her in reply, "The Holy Spirit will come upon you, and the power of the Most High will overshadow you. Therefore, the child to be born will be called holy, the Son of God. And behold, Elizabeth, your relative, has also conceived a son in her old age, and this is the sixth month for her who was called barren; for nothing will be impossible for God. Mary said, "Behold, I am the handmaid of the Lord. May it be done to me according to your word." Then the angel departed from her.

With this passage in mind we will move on to the other reflections for this mystery, explaining as we go, how God prepared Mary to be the perfect instrument for the Incarnation.

2) Who sent the angel Gabriel to Mary to ask her to consent to be His Mother.

Many today feel that Mary's role was unimportant to God's plan of salvation, but nothing could be further from the truth. Jesus came to undo the sin of Adam. We see there are many parallels between the fall at the beginning of time and our salvation. At the fall there were two people, Adam and Eve who freely disobeyed God. The Bible is clear that it was the sin of Adam that constituted "The Fall," but "the woman" was also involved. "The woman" opened the way to Adam's sin. The woman first ate the forbidden fruit and then encouraged Adam to eat the fruit. While the Bible is clear that it was Adam's sin that led to the fall of the human race; "the woman" freely consented and cooperated in his sin.

31

Our salvation in many ways is a mirror image of "The Fall." In the beginning there was a forbidden food, in our salvation there is a commanded food (the Holy Eucharist). In the beginning our first parents sinned at a tree, in salvation Jesus is "hung on a tree." In the beginning Adam was tempted in a garden, in salvation Jesus agonizes in a garden as He consents to obey the Father's Will. In the beginning "the woman" opens the way to Adam's sin, in salvation "the woman" (Mary) opens the path to the work of salvation by her fiat. As Eve freely consented to sin, Mary had to freely consent to God's plan of salvation. Adam and Eve both freely consented to sin, now in salvation Jesus (the new Adam) and Mary (the new Eve) will freely consent to be obedient to the Father's will. Eve encouraged Adam to sin, we will see Mary stand at the foot of the cross, supporting Jesus as He is "obedient unto death."

Later in the book we will more fully examine how the Bible teaches us that Mary is the new Eve, but for now it is essential to recognize that just as it took both Adam and Eve for sin to come into the world; it is now essential that both Jesus and Mary freely put themselves at the service of God's plan for the plan of salvation to come to fruition.

3) Whose Mother heard the angel say, "Hail full of grace."

4) Whose Mother was frightened by the angel and wondered what the greeting meant.

Let's take a look at the passage from Luke 1:26-38

In the sixth month, the angel Gabriel was sent from God to a town of Galilee called Nazareth, to a virgin betrothed to a man named Joseph, of the house of David, and the virgin's name was Mary. And coming to her, he said, "Hail, full of grace!

The Lord is with you." But she was greatly troubled at what was said and pondered what sort of greeting this might be. Then the angel said to her, "Do not be afraid, Mary, for you have found favor with God. Behold, you will conceive in your womb and bear a son, and you shall name him Jesus. He will be great and will be called Son of the Most High, and the Lord God will give him the throne of David his father, and he will rule over the house of Jacob forever, and of his kingdom there will be no end." But Mary said to the angel, "How can this be, since I have no relations with a man?" And the angel said to her in reply, "The Holy Spirit will come upon you, and the power of the Most High will overshadow you. Therefore, the child to be born will be called holy, the Son of God. And behold, Elizabeth, your relative, has also conceived a son in her old age, and this is the sixth month for her who was called barren; for nothing will be impossible for God." Mary said, "Behold, I am the handmaid of the Lord. May it be done to me according to your word." Then the angel departed from her.

This is no ordinary greeting. The angel addresses her with a title, "full of grace." We see in the Old Testament how names and titles were often interchangeable. In the first reading that we hear at the midnight Mass on Christmas from Is 9:5-6 we hear the following:

For a child is born to us, a son is given to us;
upon his shoulder dominion rests.
They name him Wonder-Counselor, God-Hero,
Father-Forever, Prince of Peace
His dominion is vast and forever peaceful,
Upon David's throne, and over his kingdom,
which he confirms and sustains.

33

By judgment and justice, both now and forever.
The zeal of the LORD of hosts will do this!

While this passage says, "they will call him," the fact is that "Father forever, God-hero, Wonder Counselor" are all titles for the Messiah. Here Mary is given a title by the angel. The Greek word that we translate as "Hail full of grace" implies a perfection of grace; a completeness of grace. Mary is so full of grace that there is no room for sin. This is the passage that most clearly teaches the doctrine of the Immaculate Conception, the fact that from the first moment of her existence Mary was kept safe from the poison of sin.

As we continue we will see several Old Testament realities that were prefiguring Mary. Eve was a type of Mary. The Ark of the Covenant was a type of Mary. Bethsheba, the mother of the original "son of David" (Solomon) was a type of Mary. In the next chapter we will examine how the Ark of the Covenant was pointing to Mary, but for now we want to focus on the creation of Eve. Doing this will help us grasp how the fall and salvation are in many ways a mirror image of each other. When you look in a mirror, you will notice as you raise your right hand the image raises its left hand. There is sameness, but at the same time it is opposite. The same is true when we look at the Fall and the work of our salvation.

In the beginning Eve was made without sin, in salvation Mary is made without sin (sameness). As some of the great saints have pointed out, it is foolish to think that the mother of Cain was made without sin and to believe that the Mother of Jesus was made with sin. In Genesis, Adam is put into a deep sleep and Eve is formed from his side, in salvation the body of Jesus is taken from Mary (opposite). As we continue to pray the rosary we will see this same pattern of a mirror image, sameness and opposites between the Fall and salvation throughout.

We sometimes forget that Mary was just a teenage girl, somewhere between 13-16 years old. The appearance of an angel to her had to be terrifying. This also was a mirror image of the Fall. We sometimes picture the Fall occurring because a little snake tricked Adam and Eve, but that is a misconception. The same Greek word in the Septuagint translation of the Old Testament that describes the snake in Genesis is used in the book of Revelation to describe the seven-headed dragon. The letter to the Hebrews tells us that it was "because of the fear of death" (Heb 2:14-15) that our first parents fell. The implication in Hebrews is that part of the Fall was intimidation by Satan. Satan basically said to them, "if you eat the fruit you will not die," implying that if they did not eat the fruit he would kill them. Adam should have gone to the tree of life, eaten from it, and then gotten between Satan and his bride. But that is not what he did. He allowed Satan to intimidate his bride, and when she gave him the fruit, he followed suit. Fear and a failure to trust God led to the Fall.

Now, in salvation, an angel comes to a teenage girl. She is frightened, but we will see how she chooses to put her life at the service of God's plan. In saying "yes" to God she will open the path to God becoming one of us and undoing the sin of Adam.

5) **Whose Mother heard the angel say, "Do not be afraid Mary, for you have found favor with God."**

6) **Whose Mother heard the angel say "You are to conceive a Son and name Him Jesus and He will ascend to the throne of David His Father."**

In this scene of the Bible the fact that Jesus is in the line of David is mentioned twice. We also saw in Isaiah's prophecy of the titles of the Savior, that He would be in the line of David. We will explain in the next chapter why understanding that truth is so essential to understanding what Jesus came to do. But in the meantime, we want to focus on the fact that Mary was being asked to consent to God's plan. That was not a foregone conclusion. Many of the saints speak of how all the angels waited anxiously for her response. Mary was, after all, free. As Eve freely consented to disobey God, it was necessary for Mary to freely consent to His will.

7) **Whose Mother said to the angel, "How can this be since I do not know man?"**

Many Catholic theologians have pointed out over the centuries that this is not the question you would expect Mary to ask. She was, after all, engaged to be married. The question that would make sense is, "When will this happen?" But that is not what she asked. Catholic theologians have explained through the centuries that Mary asked what she did because she had made a vow of virginity. We know the Essenes who were a prominent Jewish sect, esteemed virginity. It is believed that Mary was a part of this group. The fact that she had already made a vow of virginity would have seemed to make what the angel was saying an impossibility.

8) **Whose Mother heard the angel say, "The Holy Spirit will overshadow you, hence the child to be born will be called the Son of the Most High."**

This, of course, gives witness to the Divinity of Jesus. But it is also important to note that Mary is the first person in the New Testament to be overshadowed by the Holy Spirit. This is reminiscent of the

36

tabernacle in the desert when the Shekena cloud (the cloud of glory) covered the meeting tent (Exodus 40:34-38). It also is similar to how the Holy Spirit (again in the form of a cloud) filled the Temple at its dedication (1 Kings 8:10-11). As we go on we will see the Holy Spirit descend upon Jesus on the day of His baptism. We will see the Holy Spirit descend on the Apostles on the day of Pentecost. In the next chapter we will see Elizabeth filled with the Holy Spirit giving praise to Mary, but here we see the first person in the New Testament given this honor, Mary the Mother of God.

9) Whose Mother heard the angel say, "Elizabeth your relative has also conceived a son in her old age, and this is the sixth month for her who was called barren; for nothing will be impossible to God." (Luke 1:36-37)

Throughout the Bible we see miraculous births. Women who were too old conceiving and giving birth to babies who will become great men in salvation history. Sarah, the wife of Abraham conceiving Isaac in her 80s. In Judges 13 we read of the wife of Manoah who was barren who gave birth to the great hero Sampson. In the first book of Samuel we hear of Samuel's mother Hannah, the wife of Elkanah who was also barren, but who was also blessed with a son. And of course, in the New Testament we hear of the mother of John the Baptist who was also considered barren. In all of these births, women who were considered barren are blessed with a child.

But the conception of Jesus was even more miraculous. Never in the history of the world had a virgin conceived a child, but by the power of the Holy Spirit Mary conceives the Savior in her womb. Elizabeth's son John the Baptist will be a great man, but Mary's Son will be the Son of the Most High. Throughout the Bible great men are born in miraculous ways, but the Son of God was born of a virgin.

37

10) Whose Mother said, "I am the handmaid of the Lord, may it be done to me according to your word." (P)

Mary freely consents to be the Mother of the Savior. Again, we see the mirror image with the fall when the original "woman" freely chose to disobey God, now the new "woman" freely puts her life at the service of God's plan.

Some of the great saints spoke of how the angels waited with great expectation Mary's reply. We often think, "Of course she would say yes, who wouldn't have said yes to an angel with a message from God?" But the angles had seen person after person say "no" to God. Our first parents were told by God Himself, "Do not eat of the fruit at the center of the garden," but they ate it. Abraham was promised by God an heir, but when God was taking too long in Abraham's estimation he took matters into his own hands and sinfully conceived a child by his wife's Egyptian maidservant. God with great signs and wonders delivered the Israelites from slavery in Egypt, but in no time, they were worshipping the golden calf in the desert. God gave great wisdom to Solomon, the original "son of David" who built the Temple in Jerusalem, but as time went on his many foreign wives had turned his heart and he built places of worship for the pagan gods. God sent the prophet Isaiah to wicked King Ahaz and told him to have the king ask for a sign, any sign and God would grant it to him. So much was God willing to do to turn Ahaz from his sinful ways, but Ahaz refused to ask (Is 7:10-12). The angels had no reason to be confident that Mary would humbly put her life at the service of God's plan, but she did. As Eve opened the door for Adam to sin, Mary (the new Eve) opens the door for the Savior to come into the world.

Holy Mary, Mother of God, pray for us sinners
now and at the hour of our death. Amen.

Glory be to the Father,
and to the Son, and to the Holy Spirit:
As it was in the beginning,
is now, and ever shall be, world without end. Amen

Oh my Jesus, forgive our sins and save us from the power of hell.
Lead all souls into heaven especially those
most in need of your mercy. Amen

The Second Joyful Mystery
The Visitation

*Hail Mary, full of grace, the Lord is with you; blessed are you among women, and blessed is the fruit of your womb, **Jesus:***

1) Who made His Mother the new Ark of the Covenant. (P)

You may be wondering, where in the Visitation is the Ark of the Covenant mentioned? Again, it is essential to understand how the Old Testament is the foundation for the New. The whole Bible is about Jesus. Everything in the Old Testament was pointing to Jesus. As I pointed out in the introduction, the primary way the Old pointed to the New was through types. A type is a person place or thing in the Old that points to a person place or thing in the New.

We might first ask, why did St. Luke bother to tell the story of the Visitation? At first glance it does not seem to contain any revelation that would be necessary for our salvation. But first glances can be deceptive especially if we fail to see the connection with the Old Testament. In telling this story St. Luke wants us to hear echoes of a story from the Old Testament. The story of the Visitation mirrors the story of King David moving the Ark of the Covenant to Jerusalem. Let's take a look at the two passages, the first from 2 Sam 6: 1-12 and the second from Luke 1: 39-56, side by side (In these passages I have put a capital letter and put in "bold" the common elements. Both of these passages take place in the hill country, both have people leaping for joy, both have someone say, "Who am I that the Ark of God/ Mother of my Lord should come to me;" and in both cases, three months are mentioned).

Then David and all the people who were with him set out for Baala of Judah to bring up from there the ark of God, which bears the name "the LORD of hosts enthroned above the cherubim."

A) *They transported the ark of God on a new cart and took it away from the house of Abinadab* **on the hill.** *Uzzah and Ahio, sons of Abinadab, were guiding the cart, with Ahio walking before it,*

B) while David and all the house of Israel danced before the LORD *with all their might, with singing, and with lyres, harps, tambourines, sistrums, and cymbals... Uzzah stretched out his hand to the ark of God and steadied it, for the oxen were tipping it. Then the LORD became angry with Uzzah; God struck him on that spot, and he died there in God's presence. David was angry because the LORD's wrath had broken out against Uzzah. Therefore that place has been called Perez-uzzah even to this day. David became frightened of the LORD that day, and he said,* **C) "How can the ark of the LORD come to me?"**

A) *During those days Mary set out and traveled* **to the hill country** *in haste to a town of Judah, where she entered the house of Zechariah and greeted Elizabeth. When Elizabeth heard Mary's greeting,*

B) the infant leaped in her womb, *and Elizabeth, filled with the Holy Spirit, cried out in a loud voice and said, "Most blessed are you among women, and blessed is the fruit of your womb.*

C) And how does this happen to me, that the mother of my Lord - should come to me?

So David was unwilling to take the ark of the LORD with him into the City of David. David deposited it instead at the house of Obed-edom the Gittite.
D) *The ark of the LORD remained in the house of Obed-edom the Gittite* **for three months,** *and the LORD blessed Obed-edom and all his household.*

For at the moment the sound of your greeting reached my ears, the infant in my womb leaped for joy. Blessed are you who believed that what was spoken to you by the Lord would be fulfilled. And Mary said: "My soul proclaims the greatness of the Lord; my spirit rejoices in God savior. For he has looked upon his handmaid's lowliness; behold, from now on will all ages call me blessed. The Mighty One has done great things for me, and holy is his name. His mercy is from age to age to those who fear him. He has shown might with his arm, dispersed the arrogant of mind and heart. He has thrown down the rulers from their thrones but lifted up the lowly...The hungry he has filled with good things; the rich he has sent away empty....
D) **Mary remained with her about three months and then returned to her home.**

St. Luke in telling the story of the Visitation wants us to see that Mary is the New Ark of the Covenant. But how can that be? What similarities are there between Mary and the Ark?

The Ark of the Covenant held God's Word in stone, Mary held God's Word in the flesh. The Ark held the manna from the desert, the "bread from heaven." Mary held the true bread from heaven, Jesus in her womb (see Jn 6:51). The Ark held the staff of the high priest Aaron, but Mary held the true and eternal High Priest Himself, Jesus. The Ark of the Covenant was a type of Mary. In the introduction I pointed out how the fulfillment of the type was always greater than the original type. In the Old Testament we see the Ark was the holiest object in their faith. How much holier is Mary? We see the Ark being present when the Israelites worshipped God, so should Mary not be involved when we worship God? We see God work great miracles through the Ark when the Israelites crossed the Jordan River and when they conquered Jericho (see Jos 3:15 and Jos 6), should we not expect God to work even greater miracles through Mary?

As we continue with this Joyful Mystery we will see the parallels between these two readings more clearly.

2) Whose Mother made haste to the hill country.

Why is it important to know that this event occurred in the hill country? After all, the Bible is a book that was inspired to reveal salvific truths. Why could knowing that Mary went to the hill country to see Elizabeth be important for our salvation? It is to show that this is meant to mirror 2 Sam 6 when King David was moving the Ark to Jerusalem. It is to highlight that Mary is, in fact, the New Ark of the Covenant.

Tradition tells us that Mary herself was a miraculous birth. She was the only child of Joachim and Ann. Like Sarah (the mother of Isaac); the wife of Manoah (the mother of Sampson) and Hannah (the mother of Samuel), Ann was considered barren. So it is believed that Mary's birth was also a miraculous birth. After Mary's birth she stayed with Zechariah and Elizabeth for several years of her life. It is presumed that Mary and Elizabeth were close. In this particular mystery we see the joy of their reunification. As we continue through this set of mysteries we will see the incredible joy that God's saving work brings into the lives of the people who recognize His actions in the world.

3) Whose Mother heard Elizabeth say, "Who am I that the Mother of my Lord should come to me?"

This again mirrors the words of King David when he was speaking of the Ark of the Covenant. It is interesting that, in context, we are told that these words of Elizabeth came as she was "… filled with the Holy Spirit" (Lk 1:43). Elizabeth, while filled with the Holy Spirit declares Mary to be the Mother of the Lord. Why is this important to know? Because there are many outside the Catholic Church who argue that Mary is not important in salvation history. In their view Mary was simply the mother of His human nature, not the mother of the Divine person. Many deny that she was in fact the Mother of God. Obviously, that contradicts the teaching of St. Luke's gospel. It also contradicts biology since a mother is always the mother of a person and not just the mother of a nature. As Catholics we believe that Mary is the Mother of God just as Elizabeth declared as she was filled by the Holy Spirit.

4) Whose Mother heard Elizabeth say, "The moment your greeting reached my ears the baby leapt with joy in my womb."

44

This again mirrors 2 Samuel 6 when David and others dance for joy before the Ark. But it is also interesting to note that it was the voice of Mary that led to John the Baptist leaping for joy in his mother's womb. Luke could have said, "The baby leapt for joy the moment the Savior was brought into his presence" or "The presence of the Savior led Elizabeth's child to leap for joy;" but that it not what the Holy Spirit inspired Luke to write. It was the voice of Mary that led to the infant leaping for joy. Mary herself is a cause of joy. Mary herself is important in salvation history. Mary herself is a reason for our hope. To deny that is to ignore the teaching of the Bible.

5) Whose Mother heard Elizabeth say, "Blessed are you who believed that what was spoken to you by the Lord would be fulfilled."

Mary here is being portrayed as a woman of faith, in essence, the first disciple of the Lord. This theme of Mary being a woman of faith, a woman of prayer, the first disciple, will be taught over and over again in many ways in the scriptures. We need only to be attuned to what the Lord is teaching us as we prayerfully reflect on His plan as it is recorded in the Bible.

6) Whose Mother said, "My soul proclaims the greatness of the Lord..."

7) Whose Mother said, ".... my spirit rejoices in God my Savior."

These two reflections and the one to follow are taken from Mary song of praise often referred to as "The Magnificat." Let's take a look at the whole canticle as found in Lk 1:46-56:

And Mary said: "My soul proclaims the greatness of the Lord; my spirit rejoices in God my savior. For he has looked upon his handmaid's lowliness; behold, from now on will all ages call me blessed. The Mighty One has done great things for me, and holy is his name. His mercy is from age to age to those who fear him. He has shown might with his arm, dispersed the arrogant of mind and heart. He has thrown down the rulers from their thrones but lifted up the lowly. The hungry he has filled with good things; the rich he has sent away empty. He has helped Israel his servant, remembering his mercy, according to his promise to our fathers, to Abraham and to his descendants forever." Mary remained with her about three months and then returned to her home.

Obviously, we could offer a reflection on all of the lines of this canticle, but I have chosen to only highlight three of them. As you become more accustomed to praying the rosary in this manner you may want to use other lines from the canticle in your personal reflections. As I mentioned in the introduction, there is no one "right way" to pray the rosary in this manner.

The first reflection above is Mary's words, "My soul proclaims the greatness of the Lord." Older translations said, "My soul magnifies the Lord." How does Mary's soul proclaim God's greatness? Since the sin of Adam (and Eve) all humans were born with original sin, until Mary. Mary as we stated in the last chapter was "full of grace." The work of Jesus will usher in a "new creation." As in the original creation humans were made without sin, so it is true in the new creation and Mary is the first witness to that. She was preserved free of original sin just as Eve had been made without sin. Since Eve was a type of Mary and the Bible teaches that the glory of the Old Testament is nothing compared to the glory of the New Testament, it is only reasonable to recognize that Mary was greater than Eve from the first moment of her existence. Mary's sinless soul proclaims the greatness and love of our God.

The second reflection, "… my spirit rejoices in God my Savior" is also important for us to reflect on from an apologetics point of view. Some point to that line to say, "See, Mary needed a Savior too. Mary had to be a sinner just like the rest of us." It is true that Mary needed a Savior, but it does not follow that she also was a sinner. Mary was saved from sin from the first moment of her existence by God. Who else could have preserved her from sin? Unlike the rest of us who have the grace of salvation offered to us *after we have been tainted by sin*, Mary was preserved from sin from the first moment of her existence; in other words, she was never tainted by sin like the rest of us are. There is no contradiction between this line of the Bible and our Catholic belief in the Immaculate Conception of Mary.

8) Whose Mother said, "God has cast down the mighty from their thrones and lifted up the lowly."

As I mentioned earlier we could reflect on any of the lines of Mary's canticle and find great spiritual enrichment, but this line is one that really speaks to my heart. We Americans usually root for "the little guy." Often life seems so unfair. Oftentimes the poor are exploited by the rich; good people are taken advantage of by the unscrupulous; justice often seems to be only an elusive dream. But Mary points out that God is with the lowly and they will be lifted up by the Lord.

Mary herself is exhibit A for this. Here was a teenage girl from an insignificant little town in an insignificant little country. But we will see in the last section of this book how God will raise her to be the Queen over every emperor, king, president and prime minister. Those whom the world sees as "the important people" will often find that they were not nearly as important as they and others thought. The lowly, starting with Mary will be exalted. Justice will be done. The lowly can look to the saving work of Jesus and have hope. God is with them. They are important in the eyes of the Lord.

9) Whose Mother stayed with Elizabeth for three months and then returned home.

This is the last parallel between 2 Sam 6 and Lk 1. The Ark stayed at the house of Obed-Edom for three months and his house was blessed. Usually in the Bible when a house is blessed it implies that a child has been born. In Lk 1, the angel told Mary that her kinswoman Elizabeth was in her sixth month. Mary stayed with her for three months, at which time John would have been born. From a purely human point of view, Mary's actions do not seem to make sense. Usually a woman is in much more need of help after a child is born than before, yet in three months Mary returns home leaving Elizabeth to care for the child. St. Luke of course is highlighting that Mary was there for three months in order to highlight the parallels with 2 Samuel 6 so that his readers will recognize that Mary is in fact the new Ark of the Covenant.

10) Who made His Mother the new Ark of the Covenant. (P)

As I stated in the introduction the first and last reflection will often be the same. The primary reflection for this entire chapter is that God has made Mary the New Ark of the Covenant. As the Ark was an essential aspect of Israelite spirituality in the Old Testament, Mary is an essential aspect of spirituality in the New Covenant.

Many people outside the Catholic Church often criticize us for paying so much attention to Mary. But when we see how Mary fulfills the types of the Old Testament it will become very clear that God intends for Mary to be an important part of our spiritual lives.

Holy Mary, Mother of God, pray for us sinners
now and at the hour of our death. Amen.

Glory be to the Father,
and to the Son, and to the Holy Spirit:
As it was in the beginning,
is now, and ever shall be, world without end. Amen

Oh my Jesus, forgive our sins and save us from the power of hell.
Lead all souls into heaven especially those
most in need of your mercy. Amen

The Third Joyful Mystery
The Birth of the Savior

*Hail Mary, full of grace, the Lord is with you; blessed are you among women, and blessed is the fruit of your womb, **Jesus**:*

1) Who was born in the city of David. (P)

In the first chapter I pointed out that the Bible makes a big deal about Jesus being in the line of David. There are fifty-six times that David is mentioned in the New Testament and most of those are when the biblical writers are emphasizing that Jesus is in the line of David or when individuals refer to Him as "the Son of David."

Why is it important that Jesus is in the line of David? First it matters because the Old Testament promised that a king in the line of David would always rule the Israelites. But understanding the Kingdom of David is essential for understanding what Jesus accomplished. The Kingdom of David was a type of the Church. To understand much of Catholic belief and practice we need to understand how the kingdom of David operated.

There are two aspects in particular that we want to highlight here. First we will see in the chapters ahead how authority operated in the Old Testament kingdom. The king was the ruler, but there were other ministers who ruled with the king; other ministers who shared in the authority of the king. There were twelve ministers who oversaw various aspects of the kingdom, but one of those ministers had a very special place in the authority structure. One of the ministers was the "vicar of the king" or as we might call it today the "prime minister."

Most of the kingdoms in the ancient world were similar in that aspect of the kingdom of David. You will likely recall in the book of Genesis the story of Joseph who was sold into slavery by his brothers. Joseph eventually rose to be the number two man in the kingdom of Egypt, directly below the king himself (see Gen 41-59 to see the incredible power that Joseph attained as the prime minister of Egypt). We see that even today in England. Technically the Queen rules the nation, but the one who directs the day- to- day decisions is the prime minister. Understanding the office of "vicar' or "prime minister" in the kingdom of David will be essential for understanding the role of the pope in New Testament times. We will examine that more fully later in the book.

Another aspect of the kingdom of David, that will be essential for us to understand the plan of God, will be the role of the Queen Mother in the Old Testament. We will see later on how all the kings in the line of David brought their mother into the throne room; provided a throne for their mother; gave her a crown; and entrusted incredible authority to her. This will more fully help us understand the role of Mary in God's plan of salvation.

2) Who was born in Bethlehem, which means "house of bread." (P)

3) Who was placed in a feeding trough after His birth. (P)

Jesus was born in a town that means house of bread and then placed in a feeding trough; could God be trying to teach us something here? Is it possible that right from His birth God is trying to show us how Jesus is the "bread of life" and that we must eat this bread if we are to have eternal life?

With God there are no coincidences. One of the most prominent themes in the New Testament is the Holy Eucharist. As there was a forbidden food at the time of the Fall there is now a commanded food that is essential for our salvation. We will discuss this much more thoroughly in the Luminous Mystery chapter on the Last Supper, but for now suffice it to say that the Bible is pointing us to the Holy Eucharist from the first moments of Jesus' birth in our world.

4) **Whose parents made a difficult journey to Bethlehem when Mary was nine months pregnant.**

5) **Whose parents found no room in the Inn when they arrived in Bethlehem.**

6) **Who was born in a stable.**

When I was young I used to think how great it would be to be called by God. Imagine having a special role in God's plan of salvation. I pictured that life would always be easy, after all God would give special protection to His chosen ones-right? My attitude when I was young just showed my ignorance of scripture at the time. The truth is that God's chosen have always had very heavy crosses to bear.

God called Noah to build the Ark so that he and his family would be saved, but for the whole time he was building the Ark he was the object of laughter and ridicule. After the flood he was betrayed by his son Ham who "saw his father's nakedness" (Genesis 9:22) and then bragged to his brothers about it (translation: Ham had sexual relations with Noah's wife).

Abraham is considered the "father of faith." All Christians and Jews see themselves as "children of Abraham," but Abraham had challenge after challenge come his way. God called Abraham at the age of 75 to leave his home and go into the wilderness (Genesis 12:1-4). He needed to go into battle against four kings who captured his nephew Lot; he was promised by the Lord that he would be given a son by his wife, but that never happened until Sarah was way beyond the years of child bearing; at the age of ninety-nine Abraham had to be circumcised along with his entire household; after Isaac was born he had to drive his illegitimate son Ishmael and his mother from his home because Ishmael was persecuting Isaac; when Isaac was a young man God told him that he must offer Isaac in sacrifice to the Lord. While we can look back and see how God kept all of His promises to Abraham; Abraham certainly, at the time, faced many heart-breaking situations and had to make many leaps of faith.

The same was true for Isaac's son Jacob. He labored for seven years for his Uncle Laban who deceived him. He then had to work another seven years to receive what had originally been promised. Jacob had to flee from his twin brother Esau who was trying to kill him. Late in life his favorite son Joseph disappeared, and his other sons lied to him and said he was dead. Later he was reunited with Joseph, but he discovered the treachery of his other sons in the process.

Look at the life of Moses. He had to flee Egypt after he, in anger, had killed an Egyptian. He was called by God to return to Egypt and confront Pharaoh and to demand the release of God's people. Moses was scared to death of this! He was a wanted man in Egypt; would Pharaoh kill him? If he survived, was it likely that Pharaoh would heed his call? Moses was not a good speaker, so was it even possible that he could succeed? When he first confronted Pharaoh, the Egyptians oppress the Israelites even more than before, and people rail against Moses. After God freed the Israelites through the hand of Moses the people continually grumbled against Moses and even God. The people at one point so embittered Moses that he disobeyed God and was, as a result, not allowed to enter the Promised Land. While Moses was called to an incredibly special role in the plan of salvation there is no doubt that his life was filled with struggles and pain.

The same was true of King David. The same was true for many of the Old Testament prophets. David, time after, time faced struggles and hardships. Most of the prophets were rejected by the people they were trying to help.

In New Testament times the pattern continued. Jesus called the Apostles to be the leaders of His Church, but all but one was executed for being His disciple. The one who was not martyred (St. John) died in exile.

Mary and Joseph are a part of a long line of God's chosen who face incredible heartache and challenges. Travelling a long distance by donkey when you are nine months pregnant is not something that most women dream of doing. After that difficult journey Mary would most likely have preferred to have climbed in the hot tub at the Ramada Inn, but there was no room for her. Then to top off the humiliation her Son was born in a stable surrounded by animals; most likely not what most women dream of for the birth of their child.

Not only did they face hardships before the birth of Jesus, but afterwards they had to flee their homeland as wicked King Herod was attempting to kill their Son; they were filled with anxiety as they searched for Jesus who disappeared during the Feast of Passover in Jerusalem when He was twelve. And of course, Mary saw her Son arrested and crucified. No one who reflects on all this can possibly believe that "God's chosen" will have an easy time in life.

Why is all of this important to contemplate? God wants us to understand that He does His best work in our lives through the cross. Suffering is at the heart of God's plan of salvation. Too many people today, as they face heartaches and crosses, conclude that God does not love them; or that God just does not care about them; or that God does not exist. But in truth, the cross is a sign of God's love for us. It is through the cross that Jesus won for us the grace of salvation. It is through the cross that we have the opportunity to be co-workers with Christ (Col 1:24).

President George W. Bush once said, "When I was young and stupid, I was young and stupid." When I was young and thought that God's chosen ones would have an easy time of it, it is safe to say that I was young and stupid. The truth is that God's chosen often will have heavier crosses than the average person. We need to understand that crosses are not a sign of God's indifference to us, but rather an instrument of His love so that we can become great saints. All the great heroes of the Bible suffered greatly, we would be foolish to think that life will be easy for us.

The truth is that we can willingly accept the crosses that come our way and unite those crosses to the cross of Christ for the salvation of the world, or we can choose to allow the crosses of our lives to make us bitter, angry, resentful people. The choice is ours. The lives of Jesus and Mary show us that the cross stands at the center of God's plan of salvation. If we are to put our lives at the service of God's plan, we need to embrace those crosses, not complain about them.

7) Who was held with such great love in His Mother's arms.

Have you ever seen the love between a mother and newborn child? You can palpably feel the love! We see in Matthew 2:11 that when the

55

Magi come to Bethlehem they find the child with His Mother. There is always a special relationship between a loving mother and her child. Why is that so difficult for people to understand? And yet there are many people outside the Catholic Church who deny that Jesus and Mary have a special relationship of love. In fact, there are many people today who are hostile to the idea of devotion to Mary. But if we see how Jesus' saving work fulfills the Old Testament, then those objections will disappear.

8) Who was sung of by angels and adored by simple shepherds and great Magi.

Here we see heaven and earth come together in joy at the work of God. All types of intelligent beings recognize the Savior. The angels in heaven rejoice at His birth; simple shepherds adore: and great Magi travel great distances to bring Him gifts. The Bible is seeking to manifest that the birth of Jesus is a focal point of history. In the hierarchy of created beings, angels and then humans are at the top of the pecking order. The birth of Jesus is something that will affect all spiritual beings for the rest of eternity.

9) Whose birth was a threat to the lifestyle of King Herod.

The birth of a child changes everything. Kids can be such pesty little brats! King Herod certainly saw Jesus as a threat to his power and position. While all of the Holy Land was under the rule of the Roman Empire; Herod was the local ruler. He was known as being a ruthless man. He had killed two of his own sons which led Caesar to say that he would rather be one of Herod's pigs then one of his sons, since as a Jewish ruler he could not have contact with a pig. When Herod heard of "the newborn king" that the Magi came to honor, he was infuriated. This child had to go. He ordered the deaths of all the male children

56

two years and younger in the area of Bethlehem. This tragic event is known to history as "the slaughter of the innocents."

Unfortunately, there are many people today who see the birth of their own child as a threat to their personal lifestyle and believe it is better to slaughter their own children than to have their lifestyles destroyed. Sadly over 60 million American children have been sacrificed to the "gods of personal convenience."

Many of the women who make that choice are pressured by parents or boyfriends to end the life of their children. Many others come to repentance afterwards and are restored to friendship with the Lord. We must all celebrate when a woman recognizes her mistake and returns to the Lord. The good news of our Christian faith is that no sin of ours is greater than God's love! If you have been involved in "the slaughter of the innocents" you need only repent to receive the ever-present mercy of our Lord!

However, the people in our culture who are most like King Herod are the voters and politicians who claim to be "personally opposed to abortion" but "who can't force my morality on others." So they sit back and do nothing to protect the unborn; or worse, yet actively work so that the modern day slaughter of the innocents will continue in our land.

I am convinced that King Herod would tell you that this newborn King was a threat to the good order of the nation and that the sacrifice of the children of Bethlehem was better than the disruption and confusion this newborn King would likely bring. But there was nothing noble about what Herod did. He was a selfish political opportunist who was willing to sacrifice innocent children to hold onto power. In the same way there is no nobility in the voters or politicians of our land who are

57

"pro-choice" and allow the slaughter to continue. As Jesus says in the gospel, "If anyone has ears to hear, let him hear." (Mark 4:23).

10) Who was born in the City of David - the house of bread. (P)

We end as we began, reflecting on the fact that Jesus is a King in the line of David and that He is the Bread of Life. Those two facts are essential to understanding God's plan. Without knowing the authority structure of the kingdom of David we will not understand the authority structure that Jesus established in the Church. Without understanding how all the kings in the line of David made their mothers the Queen Mother of the kingdom we will not understand the role of Mary in the Kingdom of Jesus. And if we fail to notice that right from the very beginning of His birth, the Bible is pointing us to the Holy Eucharist, we might fail to see how the Eucharist is the "source and summit" of our faith, as the Second Vatican Council pointed out.

Holy Mary, Mother of God, pray for us sinners
now and at the hour of our death. Amen.

Glory be to the Father,
and to the Son, and to the Holy Spirit:
As it was in the beginning,
is now, and ever shall be, world without end. Amen

Oh my Jesus, forgive our sins and save us from the power of hell.
Lead all souls into heaven especially those
most in need of your mercy. Amen

The Fourth Joyful Mystery
The Presentation in the Temple

Hail Mary, full of grace, the Lord is with you; blessed are you among women, and blessed is the fruit of your womb, **Jesus***:*

1) Whose parents faithfully obeyed the laws of the Lord. (P)

This whole mystery centers around the fact that Mary and Joseph faithfully obeyed the laws of God. As we go through this mystery it will become abundantly clear that there will be times we do not understand the reason for God's commands, but that it is essential that we trust and obey Him even when we do not understand. In this mystery we will go beyond the Presentation in the Temple to examine some other facets of Jesus' early life as a child.

2) Whose parents had Him circumcised on the 8th day as the Law of the Lord required.

Why the 8th day? Why not the 7th day or the 9th day? Why not the second Sabbath after the child is born or as soon as you gather all the relatives for the celebration? Why did it have to be the 8th day? This command goes back to Abraham who lived 2,000 years before the birth of Jesus. Was God trying to teach something by having every Israelite child circumcised on the 8th day? The short answer is "yes."

We see in the story of creation that God created the world in seven days. Jesus is of course bringing about a new creation. The Apostle John highlights that in his gospel when he describes the beginning of Jesus' ministry by presenting it in a seven-day period. John is presenting a new week of creation. The 8th day of the week is actually the start of the next week. For 2,000 years God was preparing the Israelites for the new creation Jesus would establish by having every child circumcised on the 8th day. Generation after generation of Israelite circumcised their children on the 8th day as the Lord had commanded without fully knowing the significance of it.

We see the same phenomenon in the celebration of their religious feasts and other religious duties. If you search a Bible concordance you will find nineteen citations for the eighth day. Oftentimes there would be a celebration of a feast and then on the eighth day there would an even bigger celebration. The celebrations of these feasts go back to the time of Moses. For 1,500 years, through the celebration of various feasts, God was preparing the Israelites by means of the 8th day for the new creation that Jesus would bring about through His saving work.

This will also come into play when we examine how Jesus was raised on the 8th day of the week-Sunday.

3) Whose parents presented Him in the Temple on the 40th day as the law of the Lord required.

Every firstborn male child was to be presented to the Lord. Mary and Joseph are here being depicted as devout Jews who faithfully obeyed the Lord's commands.

The number 40 is of course a significant number in salvation history. Moses fasted for 40 days when he was to receive the commandments. The Israelites wandered for 40 years in the desert. Jesus begins His ministry by fasting for 40 days in the desert. And after the death and Resurrection of Jesus God gives the people of Jerusalem 40 years to come to faith and when they do not the city is destroyed. Perhaps the law of the Lord was issued to remind the Jewish people of their tendency to not trust in the Lord, which is why they wandered in the desert for 40 years. Perhaps God was preparing them for the 40 years they would have as a people to come to faith before Jerusalem was destroyed. Whatever the reason, the obedience of Mary and Joseph will give others an opportunity to give witness to the Lord, as we will see in the remaining reflections in this chapter.

4) Who was recognized by Anna who prayed day and night in the Temple.

As we examine this reflection it is important to point out that this reflection is not in biblical order. We will focus much more on the words of Simeon who gave witness to Jesus before Anna, in the next five reflections. But it is clear in the biblical text that Anna had an extensive prayer life.

Let's take a look at the big picture here. It is important that we recognize that there were many people in the Temple daily. We need to ask, why did only two people recognize God in the flesh in their presence? Reflecting on the words of Anna gives us the opportunity to see how prayer leads us to a different perspective on life. Both Anna and Simeon were very prayerful people. We are told that Anna prayed day and night in the Temple. The truth is that people who are prayerful see the world differently than people who are not devoted to prayer. Consider this passage from Lk 2: 22-38:

> *When the days were completed for their purification according to the law of Moses, they took him up to Jerusalem to present him to the Lord, just as it is written in the law of the Lord, "Every male that opens the womb shall be consecrated to the Lord," and to offer the sacrifice of "a pair of turtledoves or*

two young pigeons," in accordance with the dictate in the law of the Lord. Now there was a man in Jerusalem whose name was Simeon. This man was righteous and devout, awaiting the consolation of Israel, and the Holy Spirit was upon him. It had been revealed to him by the Holy Spirit that he should not see death before he had seen the Messiah of the Lord. He came in the Spirit into the temple; and when the parents brought in the child Jesus to perform the custom of the law in regard to him, he took him into his arms and blessed God, saying: "Now, Master, you may let your servant go in peace, according to your word, for my eyes have seen your salvation, which you prepared in sight of all the peoples, a light for revelation to the Gentiles, and glory for your people Israel." The child's father and mother were amazed at what was said about him; and Simeon blessed them and said to Mary his mother, "Behold, this child is destined for the fall and rise of many in Israel, and to be a sign that will be contradicted (and you yourself a sword will pierce) so that the thoughts of many hearts may be revealed." There was also a prophetess, Anna, the daughter of Phanuel, of the tribe of Asher. She was advanced in years, having lived seven years with her husband after her marriage, and then as a widow until she was eighty-four. She never left the temple, but worshiped night and day with fasting and prayer. And coming forward at that very time, she gave thanks to God and spoke about the child to all who were awaiting the redemption of Jerusalem.

5) **Whose parents heard Simeon say, "Now Master you can let your servant go in peace...."**

6) **Whose parents heard Simeon say, "...for my eyes have seen your salvation..."**

Like Anna, Simeon was obviously a man of deep prayer. While others in the Temple failed to recognize the Savior in their midst, Simeon proclaims that the light of the world has finally come. Because of Simeon's assertion that Jesus is the light of the world many Catholics refer to the Feast of the Presentation as Candlemas day. Again, those who are close to God see the world differently than those who are not close to the Lord.

7) **Whose parents heard Simeon say that their Son was the light to the nations and the glory of Israel.**

8) **Whose parents heard Simeon say that their Son would be the rise and the fall of many in Israel.**

Mary and Joseph had to be in awe at what was said of their Son. They of course already knew that Jesus was the Savior of the world, but Simeon and Anna reinforced that knowledge. They did not know how salvation would be brought about by their Son. They knew it was coming but did not know the when and how of it. Here in the Temple they are getting a glimpse of what is to come. The saving work of their Son would impact all nations. Their Son was the glory of Israel. Their Son would lead to many of the great ones in the land of Judah being cast down and others being raised to lofty heights. The mystery of salvation was slowly being revealed to the parents of Jesus through the words of Simeon.

9) **Whose Mother heard Simeon say that her soul would be pierced with the sword of sorrow so that the hearts of many would be laid bare.**

Any parent knows that their children are often the greatest cause of joy in their lives, but also the greatest cause of pain. The fact is that there is no greater pain in all the world than a parent experiencing the death of a child. As I explained in the introduction, I came to first really understand that the first time I saw a mother at the bedside of her dying son. For me, that was when Mary became very real.

The Bible teaches us that we are co-workers with Christ. St. Paul makes clear that our suffering is redemptive. In Col 1:24 St. Paul says,

> *Now I rejoice in my sufferings for your sake, and in my flesh*
> *I am filling up what is lacking in the afflictions of Christ on*
> *behalf of his body, which is the church...*

In Rom 8:15-17 Paul states,

> *For those who are led by the Spirit of God are children of God.*
> *For you did not receive a spirit of slavery to fall back into fear,*
> *but you received a spirit of adoption, through which we cry,*
> *"Abba Father!" The Spirit itself bears witness with our spirit*
> *that we are children of God and if children, then heirs, heirs of*
> *God and joint heirs with Christ, if only we suffer with him so*
> *that we may also be glorified with him.*

The Bible is very clear that as Christians we are called to bear the cross with Jesus! Why is that? We of course believe that we are saved by the suffering of Christ, but Christ is not done suffering! He continues to suffer through His Body on earth. He continues to suffer through you and me. As St. Paul pointed out in the quote from Colossians 1:24 we make up for what is lacking in the suffering of Christ. Now if that was not in the Bible we would think it was heresy! How could anything be lacking in the suffering of Jesus? Was Jesus incapable of bringing us salvation on His own? Of course that is not the case.

The fact is that Jesus gives us the incredible privilege to be co-workers with Him in His plan of salvation. He does not need our help, but in love, He allows us to be His co-workers. So, our suffering is redemptive. Our suffering is part of the work of Christ, since we are His Body. Our suffering can impact the salvation of ourselves and others.

If our suffering is redemptive, how much more is the suffering of Mary? The love of a mother for her child is incredible. Any mother will tell you that when their child is hurting, they feel it more acutely than when they themselves are in pain. Any loving mother would gladly take the pain of her child on herself if it would spare her child. Any mother could tell you that no one suffered more with Jesus than Mary!

So, when Jesus is a baby, Simeon gives Mary insight that suffering is in store for herself and her child. The words of Simeon point us to the fact that Mary was a co-worker with Jesus in the work of salvation.

10) Whose parents faithfully obeyed the laws of the Lord. (P)

Again, there will be times when we do not understand the laws of the Lord. In the normal course of events God is not going to come to you personally and explain why it is important that you obey. The Lord expects all of us to make a leap of faith and obey. Obedience is essential if we are to have a right relationship with the Lord.

We live in a day and age when many refuse to obey. The prevailing attitude seems to be, "No one is going to tell me what to do!" The fact is that our first parents fell because they refused to obey. Each of us needs to ask, "Am I going to follow the example of Adam and Eve, or am I going to follow the example of Mary?" In the story of the Presentation of Jesus Mary is depicted as a woman of faith who was always obedient to the laws of the Lord.

Holy Mary, Mother of God, pray for us sinners
now and at the hour of death. Amen.

Glory be to the Father,
and to the Son, and to the Holy Spirit:
As it was in the beginning,
is now, and ever shall be, world without end. Amen

Oh my Jesus, forgive our sins and save us from the power of hell.
Lead all souls into heaven especially those
most in need of your mercy. Amen

The Fifth Joyful Mystery
The Finding of the Child Jesus in the Temple

Hail Mary, full of grace, the Lord is with you; blessed are you among women, and blessed is the fruit of your womb, **Jesus:**

1) **Whose parent made great sacrifices for the practice of their faith. (P)**

2) **Whose parents brought Jesus to Jerusalem for Passover when He was twelve; as was their custom.**

As we discussed in an earlier chapter, God did not make things easy for Joseph and Mary. The practice of the Jewish faith at the time of Jesus was very demanding. Part of Jewish law was that every man was to present himself in the Temple three times a year; for the feasts of Passover, Tabernacles, and Pentecost.

For Joseph and Mary this was no ten-minute drive to the local church. Traveling in those days was difficult. It is roughly 65 miles from Nazareth to Jerusalem. Walking at a three mile an hour clip would take roughly 20 hours. We can assume that the family of Jesus would have taken a few days to walk the journey. It was a huge sacrifice for the Holy Family to go to Jerusalem several times during the year in order to be obedient to the Lord's commands.

We need to understand that the practice of the faith will require sacrifices for us as well. The first command of faith is that we love God with all our hearts, with all our souls, with all our minds and strength. That is very much different than just believing in God. The Holy Family should be a model for all of us to be willing to give of ourselves. No matter what it might take, to be faithful to the Lord's commands

3) Who was filled with zeal for His Father's house.

Let's take a look at this passage of scripture so the events are fresh within our minds. This story is told to us in Lk 2:41-52:

> Each year his parents went to Jerusalem for the feast of Passover, and when he was twelve years old, they went up according to festival custom. After they had completed its days, as they were returning, the boy Jesus remained behind in Jerusalem, but his parents did not know it. Thinking that he was in the caravan, they journeyed for a day and looked for him among their relatives and acquaintances, but not finding him, they returned to Jerusalem to look for him. After three days they found him in the temple, sitting in the midst of the teachers, listening to them and asking them questions, and all who heard him were astounded at his understanding and his answers. When his parents saw him, they were astonished, and his mother said to him, "Son, why have you done this to us? Your father and I have been looking for you with great anxiety." And he said to them, "Why were you looking for me? Did you not know that I must be in my Father's house?" But they did not understand what he said to them. He went down with them and came to Nazareth, and was obedient to them; and his mother kept all these things in her heart. And Jesus advanced [in] wisdom and age and favor before God and man.

St. John tells us of the Lord's zeal for His Father's House at the time of the cleansing of the Temple in John 2:17. But that zeal is certainly obvious here as well.

68

It is interesting that in the Bible "house" has many meanings. In 2 Sam King David indicates that he would like to build a house for the Lord, but the Prophet Nathan tells him that his heir will build the house for the Lord. But then God makes an incredible promise to David; God promises to build him a house; that is a dynasty (see 2 Sam 7:1-17). God promises that David's house will stand forever. We need to recognize that Jesus' zeal is not only for the Temple, but also for the Davidic dynasty. He is after all called many times throughout the gospels, "the Son of David." Much of what Jesus does is to fulfill the dynasty of David. The Church our Lord establishes will fulfill many of the aspects of the Davidic Dynasty.

The zeal of the Lord for His Father's House and His mission are favorite themes of mine. In fact, before Pope John Paul propagated the Luminous mysteries this was my favorite reflection on this mystery. After all, the very next mystery back then was the agony in the garden. Jesus was zealous for His Mission despite the fact that His mission required great suffering. His love for us who are saved by His passion, death and resurrection is beyond words!

4) Whose parents searched frantically for Him for three days.

We need to remember that this occurred during Passover. In this mystery Mary loses her Son for three days in Jerusalem at the time of the Passover; this is pointing us forward to when Mary will lose her Son for three days at Passover at the time of the crucifixion.

As Christians we believe that Jesus was/is sinless. Even having a perfect Son can lead to parents experiencing great pain and anxiety. And of course, none of us is perfect. For most of us our parents made incredible sacrifices for our sake. It is through the gift of parenthood that God gives us insight into His own love. As God the Father poured

Himself out in the begetting of the Son, human parents need to constantly give of themselves in love. Parenthood is one of the primary ways in this life that God helps men and women to grow in love.

As I have pointed out several times already, God did not make life easy for Joseph and Mary. We need to understand that in many ways they were like any other parents; their child was lost, and they searched for Him with great anxiety.

5) Who amazed all those in the Temple with the Wisdom of His questions and answers.

Jesus was zealous for His Father's plan. Here we see Jesus as a child go to His Father's House and discuss the great mysteries of faith. We have seen how all in the Temple were amazed at His insights into the word of God.

6) Who heard His Mother say, "Son, why have you done this to us? Your father and I have been searching for you with great anxiety."

7) Who said to His Mother, "Why were you searching for me? Did you not know that I must be in my Father's house?"

Think for a moment of all that had taken place in Mary's life up to this point with her Son. An angel came to her and asked her to be the mother of the Savior; she gave birth to God in the flesh; the shepherds had told her of the message of the angle about the birth of the Savior; Magi from the east came to pay Him homage; Simeon proclaimed that her Son would be the light to the nations and the glory of Israel and that her Son would be the rise and the fall of many in Israel. And yet there is still so much mystery for her in God's plan. If anyone should have had perfect knowledge of God's plan it was Mary, but she did not.

I often think of this when I discuss faith with people who are so certain that on their own the Holy Spirit will guide them to personally know all the truths of the Christian faith. There are many who are certain that they do not have to listen to the Church, or scholars, or pastors. They are certain that they personally have the Holy Spirit and they need to listen to no one else.

The fact is, and we will examine this when we get to the glorious mysteries, the promise of Jesus that the Holy Spirit will guide us to all truth is a promise to the Church, not a promise to every individual Christian. We can certainly study the Bible and pray over the scriptures with great spiritual benefit, but we need to be humble enough to recognize that we might personally be wrong about certain aspects of God's plan of salvation. In later chapters we will reflect on how we can personally come to know God's saving truth, but for now it is important to acknowledge that on our own we might not individually understand the fullness of God's plan. If Mary sometimes did not understand the full plan, we had better be humble enough to see that we might not personally always understand either.

8) Who returned to Nazareth with Joseph and Mary and was obedient to them. (Luke 2:51) (P)

This is a mystery that we could reflect on for our entire lives and still marvel at what is being said. Jesus is the all -powerful God and yet He was obedient to His earthly parents! God obeyed people! Wow!

In this, Jesus is a model for every child on the face of the earth. If, when God became one of us, He chose to be obedient to His parents;

do you not think that He expects us mere mortals to be obedient to our parents?

In addition to children, He is a model for all of us. I know I personally find it difficult to be obedient to my Bishop even though I made a vow to do just that. I sometimes resent some of the stupid laws of our nation, or state, or local community. What do you think God wants me to do? If He was obedient to a mere man and woman, do you not think that He wants me to be obedient to legitimate authority?

I often hear people say, "the Catholic Church has too many rules, I want to be free to follow my own plans." As I stated earlier we will examine more carefully the issue of authority when we get to the Glorious mysteries, but for now it is important to understand that the Lord wants us to be obedient to legitimate authority. In Psalm 81: 12-13 the Lord addresses the stubbornness of heart that so often leads people to go their own way rather than being faithful members of His people:

> *But my people did not listen to my words;*
> *Israel would not submit to me.*
> *So I thrust them away to the hardness of their heart;*
> *Let them walk in their own machinations*

In the Bible, God allowing us to go our own way is seen as a punishment from Him. If Jesus could be obedient to the legitimate authority "over Him" in family life, you better believe that He wants us to be obedient to the legitimate authorities over us.

9) Whose Mother pondered all these things in her heart.

Mary is portrayed as a model of prayer for us. This is the second time that we are told that Mary pondered her experiences in her heart (the first was in Luke 2:19 when the shepherds came to Bethlehem after the angel appeared to them). God certainly wants us to see in these passages that Mary is a woman of prayer whom we should imitate.

10) Whose parents made great sacrifices for the practice of their faith. (P)

The reason God created us, the reason we have life, is to come to know, love and serve God. Faith is not meant to be a casual aspect of our lives that we can focus on when it is convenient for us. Faith is what our lives are all about. Faith is what gives us the hope of eternal life. Mary and Joseph are wonderful examples for us in the practice of the faith. The Lord calls each of us into a strong personal relationship with Him. If the Lord is to be at the center of our lives we, like Joseph and Mary will need to make great sacrifices in the practice of our faith.

Holy Mary, Mother of God, pray for us sinners
now and at the hour of our death. Amen.

Glory be to the Father,
and to the Son, and to the Holy Spirit:
As it was in the beginning,
is now, and ever shall be, world without end. Amen

Oh my Jesus, forgive our sins and save us from the power of hell.
Lead all souls into heaven especially those
most in need of your mercy. Amen.

Section 2

The

Luminous

Mysteries

The First Luminous Mystery
The Baptism of Jesus

Hail Mary, full of grace, the Lord is with you; blessed are you among women, and blessed is the fruit of your womb, **Jesus:**

1) Who first revealed the Trinity on the day of His baptism. (P)

In the Old Testament there were hints that God was more than a solitary figure, but at the Baptism of Jesus is when we see for the first time the Father, Son and Holy Spirit revealed. In Gen 1:26-27 we read:

> *Then God said: Let* **us** *make human beings in* **our** *image, after our likeness. Let them have dominion over the fish of the sea, the birds of the air, the tame animals, all the wild animals, and all the creatures that crawl on the earth. God created mankind in* **His** *image in the image of God* **He** *created them; male and female* **He** *created them.*

Here we have hints of plurality in God. He says, "Let **us** (plural) make man in **our** (plural) image. In the Divine image **He** (singular) made them; male and female **He** (singular) made them." We also see hints in the Wisdom literature when the Bible describes Wisdom in divine terms, but Wisdom is feminine and is clearly not the same person as the Father. While there were hints in the Old Testament that God is not a solitary figure, this is the first time that we see Father, Son and Holy Spirit together. Let's take a look at the passage in Matthew 3:13-17:

> *Then Jesus came from Galilee to John at the Jordan to be baptized by him. John tried to prevent him, saying, "I need to be baptized by you, and yet you are coming to me?" Jesus said*

75

to him in reply, "Allow it now, for thus it is fitting for us to fulfill all righteousness." Then he allowed him. After Jesus was baptized, he came up from the water and behold, the heavens were opened [for Him], and he saw the Spirit of God descending like a dove [and] coming upon Him. And a voice came from the heavens, saying, "This is my beloved Son, with whom I am well pleased."

We see the three Persons of the Trinity revealed: the Son goes to John, the Holy Spirit descends on Him in the form of a dove and the voice of the Father speaks.

2) Who chose to become the "Christ" through the ministry of the Levite, John the Baptist. (P)

The word "Christ" means the anointed one. This is the Greek word for the Hebrew word "Messiah". The Old Testament tells us that the Savior will be the anointed of God. And His anointing comes through the ministry of John the Baptist. The father of John was a priest, so John was definitely of the tribe of Levi (the priestly tribe). He was most likely a priest (like father like son). And Jesus chose to become the Messiah or Christ through John's ministry. Why did Jesus need the ministry of another person to become the Christ?

Jesus of course is God and He needs no one. If anyone could have said to the Father, "Father just send the Holy Spirit to anoint me" it was Jesus. IF anyone could have said, "Come Holy Spirit and anoint me now" it was Jesus. If anyone could have said, "I don't need to go to some man to receive this grace—I'll just go to God" it was Jesus. So why did He choose to become the Christ through the ministry of a mere man? Because He wanted to show us how we need others. Just as

76

God is a community of love; God made us to be community. He wants us to know that we need one another.

In God's plan it is not enough for us to have a personal relationship with Him. Please do not get me wrong. We need to have a personal relationship with Him, but that is not enough. He wants us to be a community of love, so He made us so that we need one another.

I have often heard people say, "Why do I need to confess to a priest when I can go right to God?" We will later in the book address the issue of the ministerial priesthood, but for now it is essential that we recognize that in order for us to receive the grace of salvation, we need others. Jesus chose to become the Christ through the ministry of John the Baptist; He wants us to be humble enough to go to others in order to receive His saving grace.

3) Who heard John the Baptist say, "Behold the Lamb of God…"

4) Who heard John the Baptist say, "….the Lamb who takes away the sins of the world."

We need to turn to see how St. John reports the Baptism of the Lord in his gospel; the following is from John 1:29-34:

> *The next day he (John the Baptist) saw Jesus coming toward him and said, "Behold, the Lamb of God, who takes away the sin of the world. He is the one of whom I said, 'A man is coming after me who ranks ahead of me because he existed before me.' I did not know Him, but the reason why I came baptizing with water was that he might be made known to Israel." John testified further, saying, "I saw the Spirit come down like a dove from the sky and remain upon Him. I did not*

77

know Him, but the one who sent me to baptize with water told me, 'On whomever you see the Spirit come down and remain, He is the one who will baptize with the Holy Spirit.' Now I have seen and testified that He is the Son of God."

To understand what is going on here it is necessary to understand the Old Testament. There are two different events that need to be examined; the first is the story of the sacrifice of Isaac by Abraham, the second is the original Passover meal when the Israelites were slaves in Egypt.

First the sacrifice of Isaac by Abraham which we read of in Gen 22:1-18:

Sometime afterward, God put Abraham to the test and said to him: Abraham! "Here I am!" he replied. Then God said: Take your son Isaac, your only one, whom you love, and go to the land of Moriah. There offer him up as a burnt offering on one of the heights that I will point out to you. Early the next morning Abraham saddled his donkey, took with him two of his servants and his son Isaac, and after cutting the wood for the burnt offering, set out for the place of which God had told him.

On the third day Abraham caught sight of the place from a distance. Abraham said to his servants: "Stay here with the donkey, while the boy and I go on over there. We will worship and then come back to you." So Abraham took the wood for the burnt offering and laid it on his son Isaac, while he himself carried the fire and the knife. As the two walked on together, Isaac spoke to his father Abraham. "Father!" he said. "Here I am," he replied. Isaac continued, "Here are the fire and the wood, but where is the sheep for the burnt offering?" "My

78

son," Abraham answered, "God will provide the sheep for the burnt offering." Then the two walked on together.

When they came to the place of which God had told him, Abraham built an altar there and arranged the wood on it. Next he bound his son Isaac, and put him on top of the wood on the altar. Then Abraham reached out and took the knife to slaughter his son. But the angel of the LORD called to him from heaven, "Abraham, Abraham!" "Here I am," he answered. "Do not lay your hand on the boy," said the angel. "Do not do the least thing to him. For now I know that you fear God, since you did not withhold from me your son, your only one." Abraham looked up and saw a single ram caught by its horns in the thicket. So Abraham went and took the ram and offered it up as a burnt offering in place of his son. Abraham named that place Yahweh-yireh; hence people today say, "On the mountain the LORD will provide." A second time the angel of the LORD called to Abraham from heaven and said: "I swear by my very self that because you acted as you did in not withholding from me your son, your only one, I will bless you and make your descendants as countless as the stars of the sky and the sands of the seashore; your descendants will take possession of the gates of their enemies, and in your descendants all the nations of the earth will find blessing, because you obeyed my command."

Here we have a loving father who is willing to be obedient to God for the salvation of the world. For three days in Abraham's mind his son was as good as dead, but Abraham chose to obey. Isaac carried the wood for the sacrifice, just as Jesus will later carry the wood of the cross for His own sacrifice. They rode a donkey to the place of sacrifice just as Jesus rode a donkey into Jerusalem for His sacrifice.

Isaac said, "Father here is the wood and here is the fire, but where is the sacrifice?" And Abraham said, "God will provide the lamb." Jesus of course is the Lamb that God provides. This whole incident is pointing us to the saving work of Christ, but here God saves Isaac from being killed. In our salvation God really does have His beloved Son lay down His life for the salvation of the world.

This incident occurred near the town of Salem. Later, when the word for "the Lord will provide" (Genesis 22:14) is put in front of the name of this town it will become Jerusalem. Yes, this sacrifice of Isaac was to take place near where the sacrifice of Jesus took place. And of course, we believe that God kept His promise and provided the Lamb of God for the saving sacrifice, Jesus. This whole incident is meant to be a type of the sacrifice of Jesus, but we will examine that more in a later chapter.

The other Old Testament story that sheds light on the point John the Baptist is making goes to the story of the original Passover meal and how God saved the Israelites from their slavery. Look at the key passage in Ex 12:1-14:

> *The LORD said to Moses and Aaron in the land of Egypt: This month will stand at the head of your calendar; you will reckon it the first month of the year. Tell the whole community of Israel: On the tenth of this month every family must procure for itself a lamb, one apiece for each household. If a household is too small for a lamb, it along with its nearest neighbor will procure one, and apportion the lamb's cost in proportion to the number of persons, according to what each household consumes. Your lamb must be a year-old male and without blemish. You may take it from either the sheep or the goats. You will keep it until the fourteenth day of this month, and then,*

80

with the whole community of Israel assembled, it will be slaughtered during the evening twilight. They will take some of its blood and apply it to the two doorposts and the lintel of the houses in which they eat it. They will consume its meat that same night, eating it roasted with unleavened bread and bitter herbs. Do not eat any of it raw or even boiled in water, but roasted, with its head and shanks and inner organs. You must not keep any of it beyond the morning; whatever is left over in the morning must be burned up.

This is how you are to eat it: with your loins girt, sandals on your feet and your staff in hand, you will eat it in a hurry. It is the LORD's Passover. For on this same night I will go through Egypt, striking down every firstborn in the land, human being and beast alike, and executing judgment on all the gods of Egypt—I, the LORD! But for you the blood will mark the houses where you are. Seeing the blood, I will pass over you; thereby, when I strike the land of Egypt, no destructive blow will come upon you. This day will be a day of remembrance for you, which your future generations will celebrate with pilgrimage to the LORD; you will celebrate it as a statute forever.

When John the Baptist referred to Jesus as the "Lamb of God" he was saying a lot. We need to bring the words of Abraham that, "God will provide the Lamb" and the whole Passover liturgy to mind if we are to understand what is being proclaimed about Jesus.

In the story of Abraham and Isaac, Abraham made the point that the Lamb which would save "the children of Abraham" would be provided by God Himself, but the Lamb would of course be sacrificed.

81

In the Passover liturgy we see that the lamb had to be one year old (that is in the prime of life); it had to be male; it had to be without blemish; it would then be killed, and its blood put on the doorpost and lintel of the home; and the blood of the lamb would save the Israelites. But what will be especially important when we discuss the Holy Eucharist is that they had to eat the lamb (Ex 12:7)! If they failed to eat the lamb the firstborn son in their family would not have been saved.

Knowing all this background is essential to understanding how the Old Testament was pointing to Jesus and would be fulfilled by Him. As the blood of the lamb saved the Israelites on that original Passover, the blood of Jesus will save us now. As the original Passover required a male lamb, without blemish and in the prime of life, Jesus is of course male, He is without sin and He was crucified in the prime of life. As the Passover led to the Israelites being set free from their slavery in Egypt, Jesus, the Lamb of God will set us free from our slavery to sin.

5) Who heard John the Baptist say, "You should be baptizing me, I should not be baptizing you."

John recognized that the role of Jesus was far more important in God's plan of salvation than his own role. He calls Jesus, "the Son of God." We do not know if John fully understood what he was asserting, but there is no doubt that John in humility recognized that Jesus was not just another man and was more important than himself.

6) Who said to John, "We must do this to fulfill all righteousness."

7) Who would later teach, "Amen, amen, I say to you, no one can enter the Kingdom of God without being born of water and Spirit."

It is essential to see these two teachings of Jesus as going hand in hand. What does "all righteousness" mean? In being baptized, Jesus was transforming baptism into a sacrament of the new covenant. He later teaches in John 3:5 that we need to be baptized if we are to enter into His Kingdom. Jesus asserts this as He teaches Nicodemus what is necessary for salvation, but we see immediately after He finishes speaking to Nicodemus that He and the Apostles go out baptizing (John 3:22).

We see parallels between the Baptism of Jesus and our own baptism. Jesus is baptized in water, we are baptized in water; the Holy Spirit descends upon Him, the Holy Spirit descends upon us; the voice of the Father declares Jesus is His Son (by nature) in whom He is well pleased, we are declared a son or daughter of God (by adoption). In being baptized Jesus begins His ministry. In our baptism we begin our new life in the family of God. Jesus needed to be baptized to transform baptism into the sacrament of renewal for us. We need to be baptized to receive the grace Jesus won for us through His cross and Resurrection.

8) Who was anointed by the Holy Spirit in the form of a dove.

Why a dove? Why not an eagle? Why not a hawk or a raven? Why not a myriad of angels in visible form swooping down from heaven? Because God wanted us to remember a story from the Old Testament that was pointing to Baptism: the story of Noah, the Ark, the great flood, and a dove that flew above the waters that washed away sin and preserved goodness. Let's take a look at part of that story from Gen 8:8-12:

> *Then he released a dove, to see if the waters had lessened on the earth. But the dove could find no place to perch, and it returned to him in the ark, for there was water over all the earth. Putting out his hand, he caught the dove and drew it back to him inside the ark. He waited yet seven days more and again released the dove from the ark. In the evening the dove came back to him, and there in its bill was a plucked-off olive leaf! So Noah knew that the waters had diminished on the earth. He waited yet another seven days and then released the dove; but this time it did not come back.*

In telling us in John's gospel that the Holy Spirit descended on Jesus in the form of a dove, the biblical writer wants us to read back into the Old Testament the presence of the Holy Spirit over the waters of the great flood. Why? Just as through water and the Holy Spirit God brought about a new creation in the days of Noah, He wants us to recognize that we become a new creation by water and the Holy Spirit on the day of our baptism. Just as the great flood washed away sin and preserved goodness; God washes away our sin and preserves the goodness in us when we are baptized.

9) Who heard the voice of the Father say, "This is my beloved Son in whom I am well pleased."

Jesus of course is the eternal Son of God, He did not become God's Son on the day of His baptism. The Father simply publicly declares the eternal truth of who Jesus is. We, on the other hand, are not by nature children of God; by nature we are servants of God. There is nothing we could do on our own to become God's children. The "good news" is that we are not on our own; we have a Savior. When we follow Jesus into the waters of baptism we are united to Him. Through our union with Him we become sons and daughters of God in the One eternal Son.

10) Who first revealed the Trinity on the day of His Baptism. (P)

We finish where we began, with the revelation that God is a community of love that we call "The Trinity." This revelation of God is essential for us to understand ourselves since we are made in the image and likeness of God. As God is not a solitary individual we are not meant to be rugged individualists; we are meant to be members of a community of love. That is why we are meant to be born into a community of love that we call the family. In God's plan, a man and woman are united to become one (as God is one), and the love that unites them is so strong, so real, so tangible that nine months later you can give that love a name. In God's plan of creation, each one of us is meant to be love come to life. The human family is meant to point us to God who is, in essence, the Divine Family.

Understanding that God is a community of love is also essential for understanding God's plan of salvation. Just as in creating us He made it so that we would be born into a family; in saving us we are meant to be born into His Family—the Church. It is not enough that we have a personal relationship with God; we also must be united to one another as a community. Without community we cannot image God in the world because God is a community of love.

Holy Mary, Mother of God, pray for us sinners
now and at the hour of our death. Amen.

Glory be to the Father,
and to the Son, and to the Holy Spirit:
As it was in the beginning,
is now, and ever shall be, world without end. Amen

Oh my Jesus, forgive our sins and save us from the power of hell.
Lead all souls into heaven especially those
most in need of your mercy. Amen

The Second Luminous Mystery
The Wedding Feast of Cana

Hail Mary, full of grace, the Lord is with you; blessed are you among women, and blessed is the fruit of your womb, **Jesus:**

1) Who chose to first manifest His glory through the intercession of Mary. (P)

Think of all the miracles that Jesus performed. Think of all the opportunities that Jesus had to manifest His power, why did He choose to first manifest His glory at Mary's behest? We will see in later chapters the role of the Queen Mother in the kingdom of David and how the Queen Mother would intercede with her son the king on behalf of citizens of the kingdom. Here, the Mother of the King of kings intercedes on behalf of this young couple.

Also present here is a parallel with the Fall in the book of Genesis. In Genesis "the woman" leads Adam into sin. In the story of the Cana wedding Mary, the new "woman" leads Jesus the new Adam to first manifest His glory.

Let's take a look at the first miracle of the Lord in John 2:1-11:

> *On the third day there was a wedding in Cana in Galilee, and the mother of Jesus was there. Jesus and his disciples were also invited to the wedding. When the wine ran short, the mother of Jesus said to him, "They have no wine." [And] Jesus said to her, "Woman, how does your concern affect me? My hour has not yet come." His mother said to the servers, "Do whatever he tells you." Now there were six stone water jars*

there for Jewish ceremonial washings, each holding twenty to thirty gallons. Jesus told them, "Fill the jars with water." So they filled them to the brim. Then he told them, "Draw some out now and take it to the headwaiter." So they took it. And when the headwaiter tasted the water that had become wine, without knowing where it came from (although the servers who had drawn the water knew), the headwaiter called the bridegroom and said to him, "Everyone serves good wine first, and then when people have drunk freely, an inferior one; but you have kept the good wine until now." Jesus did this as the beginning of his signs in Cana in Galilee and so revealed his glory, and his disciples began to believe in him.

As we continue to reflect on this mystery the OT parallels will become more evident.

2) Who chose to first manifest His glory at a wedding banquet.

Throughout the NT Jesus is portrayed as the bridegroom and His Church as His bride. The whole plan of God is a love relationship between Him and His people. There are twelve references to bridegrooms in the NT and fourteen references to weddings. In Matthew 22 we are told the parable of the king who throws a wedding banquet for his son. This is a rather clear reference to the celebration of the Eucharist in the new covenant of love.

We see throughout the OT God refers to His relationship with His people in terms of bridegroom and bride. In Jewish wedding customs a man and woman were considered married during the engagement period. It was only after the ceremony however, that they would move in together and have children. The OT period can be considered the engagement period. We see numerous references to this bridegroom –

bride relationship in the OT. See Is 54:5-10, Jer2:1-2, 33:10-17, and Ez 16:8. In addition to these positive references we see God accuse His people of adultery as well. See Hos 1:2-3, 2:15-20, Jer 2:32 &3:20, Ez 16:15-22 & 32.

In the Book of Revelation, the wedding banquet of the Lamb is also a clear reference to the marital image of Jesus and His bride, the Church. It is clear throughout the NT that Jesus wills His people to be in a relationship of love with Him. So, it is only appropriate that Jesus would first manifest His glory at a celebration of love. In fact, the wedding at Cana is pointing us to God's plan of a nuptial banquet with His people.

In short, throughout the OT God promises to take Israel as His bride. In today's terms the OT is the time of engagement, but in Jesus the wedding is consummated. In the wedding feast of Cana, we see a prefiguring of the wedding of the Lamb.

3) Whose mother Mary was invited to a wedding feast in Cana of Galilee; Jesus and His disciples were also invited.

Why does John mention that Mary was invited to the wedding banquet, before saying that Jesus was invited? In all honesty I have no idea. I include this reflection for apologetic purposes. In dialoging about scripture with some non-Catholics I have often heard them argue that Peter had no position of primacy because in Galatians 2:9 James is mentioned before Peter (rendered as Cephas in Galatians). Some I've been in dialogue with have said, "If Peter was so important, why did Paul mention James first? Obviously, Peter was not so important as you make him out to be." It is however obvious to all followers of Christ that Jesus is far more important in salvation history than Mary is. And yet John mentions Mary was invited to the wedding in Cana before he mentions that Jesus was invited. This merely demonstrates that the most important person is not always mentioned first in the Bible.

4) Who heard His Mother say, "They have no wine."

Here we see Mary's love and compassion; she is concerned about the well- being of this newlywed couple. So Mary intercedes on their behalf. We will see later that Jesus has made His Mother a powerful intercessor for His people.

5) Who said to His Mother, "Woman, what's this between you and me?"

I remember one time I was working a summer job for my father's company. We were waiting for the backhoe operator to finish his work so we could do ours when the leader of my work crew said to the foreman of the company where we were working, "Jay here is going to be a priest." The man's eyes got big with surprise and he asked me, "A Catholic priest?" When I responded in the affirmative he said, "Oh, God doesn't like you Catholics! The way you worship Mary is very offensive to Him." I informed him that we do not worship Mary, but we do hold her in very high esteem. He responded, "Yes you do; and besides, Jesus didn't even like her." I was, needless to say, shocked by this claim and said, "What do you mean He didn't like her?" The man responded, "What did He call her from the cross? He called her woman! I would never call my mother that! He was putting her in her place. He was telling her that she's not important. Why else would He call her woman?"

In all honesty at the time I did not know why Jesus called His Mother woman, although I was pretty sure that, as Jesus was dying on the cross for my sins and yours, He did not look down on His Mother and break the 4th commandment by insulting her! So why did He call her woman?

He called her "woman" because He was saying that she is the "new Eve." When we look back at Genesis we see that before sin came into the world Adam referred to the lady in the garden with him as "woman." It was only after sin came into the world that he named her "Eve." *Before sin he shared his name with her; he was "man" she was "woman."* It is only after sin came into the world that he named her as he had named the animals. After sin there was a disparity between them, but before sin there was a shared dignity.

In Genesis "the woman" led Adam into sin. In the NT Jesus is portrayed as the "new Adam" (see Rom 5:14). In Genesis "the woman" led Adam into sin; so at the wedding feast of Cana the new "woman" leads the "new Adam" to manifest His glory. Eve chose to disobey God and brought death and sin into the world; Mary, on the other hand, put her life at the service of God's plan leading to the "new Adam" conquering sin and death. So both on the cross and at the wedding feast of Cana Jesus is pointing us to the truth that Mary is the new Eve.

Some point to Jesus' words at the wedding feast, "What's this between you and me?" as some kind of an insult. In reality Jesus was using a Jewish idiom that basically means, "I know you're going to ask me to do something; and you know that I don't want to do it, but because of the relationship we have, I will do what you ask." We see the same basic phrase in Matthew 8:29 and parallel passages when the demons say to Jesus, "What's this between you and us?" They know Jesus has authority over them; they know Jesus is going to tell them to do something they do not want to do; they know that they will need to obey Him. So at the wedding feast of Cana Jesus did not intend to do anything about the wine situation, but because Mary interceded we see Him perform His first miracle.

6) Who said to His Mother, "My hour has not yet come."

I used to believe that Jesus was basically saying that His time to perform miracles had not yet arrived, but I was wrong. John uses the term "hour" in reference to the time of Jesus' passion, death and resurrection. In John 7:30 and again in John 8:20 we see the enemies of Jesus attempting to seize Him but being unable to because His "hour" had not yet come. It is not until John 12:30 that Jesus says, "The hour has come," but we see numerous miracles performed by Jesus between the wedding Feast of Cana and John 12. From John 12:30 we see the events leading up to and including His passion, death and resurrection.

But that leaves the question, why did Jesus say, "My hour has not yet come" when told about the need for wine at the wedding feast? It certainly implies that "wine" will have a central place in Jesus' hour. As we go on we'll see how Jesus transforms wine to become His Blood, the Blood of the new and everlasting covenant, at the Last Supper. It is through the "Paschal Mystery" (that is, the gift of the Holy Eucharist at the Last Supper, the Passion, death and Resurrection), that the "Wedding of the Lamb" will take place. In saying, "My hour has not yet come" He is pointing us to His saving work which includes wine becoming His Sacred Blood at the Last Supper.

7) Whose Mother said to the servants, "Do whatever He tells you to do."

As I implied earlier, there are some people who try to explain away Mary's intercession here by claiming that Jesus was insulting her. I have actually had people tell me that Jesus' saying to His Mother, "What's this between you and me" was an insult to Mary; basically, telling her to "butt out." That interpretation is pretty far-fetched as we see Jesus doing precisely what Mary's intercession would have led Him to do.

In going to the servants and telling them to do what Jesus tells them to do, we see Mary's faith in Her Son and her certainty that her intercession would be fruitful. These words of Mary are, interestingly enough, the last words we hear from Mary in the Bible. "Do whatever He tells you to do" is Mary's message to all the world; she wants all of us to obey her Son.

8) Who presented the finest wine after a lesser had been served.

Is St. John telling us that every other married couple in history was cheated at their wedding because they didn't have wine made by Jesus Himself? Possibly, but doubtful. After all, knowing how good the wine was is not something important to know for our salvation. St. John was actually comparing the Old Covenant with the New. The Old Covenant was good, but the New is far better. The Old Covenant was a relationship with God Himself, but the New brings the consummation. The relationship between God and His people is far deeper, far more intimate, is much greater than the relationship in the Old Covenant. In the OT we have the engagement, in the NT we have the wedding.

9) Whose disciples began to believe in Him after the miracle.

10) Whose Mother believed in Him before the miracle; it was her faith that led to the miracle. (P)

Here, Mary is portrayed as "the first disciple." She believed in Jesus before anyone else. Her faith and the miracle her faith brought about led others to believe in Jesus. As we go on we will see how Mary's faith continues to lead others to believe in her Son.

*Holy Mary, Mother of God, pray for us sinners
now and at the hour of our death. Amen.*

*Glory be to the Father,
and to the Son, and to the Holy Spirit:
As it was in the beginning,
is now, and ever shall be, world without end. Amen*

*Oh my Jesus, forgive us our sins and save us from the power of hell.
Lead all souls to heaven, especially those most
most in need of your mercy. Amen.*

94

The Third Luminous Mystery
The Preaching of the Kingdom

Hail Mary, full of grace, the Lord is with you; blessed are you among women, and blessed is the fruit of your womb, **Jesus:**

1) Whose first sermon was, "Repent for the Kingdom of God is at hand." (P)

Notice that Jesus did not say, "2,000 years from now, after the Rapture, I'll come again and establish a Kingdom." No, He preaches that the Kingdom is an imminent event. This certainly would be in keeping with the expectations of the Jewish people of the time. Based primarily on the Prophet Daniel, the Jewish people expected the Messiah at the time of Jesus.

Let's take a look at Daniel 2:1-45:

> *In the second year of his reign, King Nebuchadnezzar had a dream which left his spirit no rest and robbed him of his sleep. So he ordered that the magicians, enchanters, sorcerers, and Chaldeans be summoned to interpret the dream for him. When they came and presented themselves to the king, he said to them, "I had a dream which will allow my spirit no rest until I know what it means." The Chaldeans answered the king in Aramaic: "O king, live forever! Tell your servants the dream and we will give its meaning." The king answered the Chaldeans, "This is what I have decided: unless you tell me the dream and its meaning, you shall be cut to pieces and your houses made into a refuse heap. But if you tell me the dream and its meaning, you shall receive from me gifts and presents*

and great honors. Therefore tell me the dream and its meaning."

Again they answered, "Let the king tell his servants the dream and we will give its meaning." But the king replied: "I know for certain that you are bargaining for time, since you know what I have decided. If you do not tell me the dream, there can be but one decree for you. You have conspired to present a false and deceitful interpretation to me until the crisis is past. Tell me the dream, therefore, that I may be sure that you can also give its correct interpretation."

The Chaldeans answered the king: "There is not a man on earth who can do what you ask, O king; never has any king, however great and mighty, asked such a thing of any magician, enchanter, or Chaldean. What you demand, O king, is too difficult; there is no one who can tell it to the king except the gods, who do not dwell among people of flesh." At this the king became violently angry and ordered all the wise men of Babylon to be put to death. When the decree was issued that the wise men should be slain, Daniel and his companions were also sought out.

Then Daniel prudently took counsel with Arioch, the chief of the king's guard, who had set out to kill the wise men of Babylon. He asked Arioch, the officer of the king, "What is the reason for this harsh order from the king?" When Arioch told him, Daniel went and asked for time from the king, that he might give him the interpretation.

Daniel went home and informed his companions Hananiah, Mishael, and Azariah, that they might implore the mercy of the

God of heaven in regard to this mystery, so that Daniel and his companions might not perish with the rest of the wise men of Babylon. During the night the mystery was revealed to Daniel in a vision, and he blessed the God of heaven:

"Blessed be the name of God forever and ever, for wisdom and power are his. He causes the changes of the times and seasons, establishes kings and deposes them. He gives wisdom to the wise and knowledge to those who understand. He reveals deep and hidden things and knows what is in the darkness, for the light dwells with him. To you, God of my ancestors, I give thanks and praise, because you have given me wisdom and power. Now you have shown me what we asked of you, you have made known to us the king's dream." So Daniel went to Arioch, whom the king had appointed to destroy the wise men of Babylon, and said to him, "Do not put the wise men of Babylon to death. Bring me before the king, and I will tell him the interpretation of the dream." Arioch quickly brought Daniel to the king and said, "I have found a man among the Judean exiles who can give the interpretation to the king." The king asked Daniel, whose name was Belteshazzar, "Can you tell me the dream that I had and its meaning?" In the king's presence Daniel made this reply:

"The mystery about which the king has inquired, the wise men, enchanters, magicians, and diviners could not explain to the king. But there is a God in heaven who reveals mysteries, and he has shown King Nebuchadnezzar what is to happen in the last days; this was your dream, the visions you saw as you lay in bed. To you in your bed there came thoughts about what should happen in the future, and he who reveals mysteries showed you what is to be. To me also this mystery has been

revealed; not that I am wiser than any other living person, but in order that its meaning may be made known to the king, that you may understand the thoughts of your own mind.

"In your vision, O king, you saw a statue, very large and exceedingly bright, terrifying in appearance as it stood before you. Its head was pure gold, its chest and arms were silver, its belly and thighs bronze, its legs iron, its feet partly iron and partly clay. While you watched, a stone was hewn from a mountain without a hand being put to it, and it struck its iron and clay feet, breaking them in pieces. The iron, clay, bronze, silver, and gold all crumbled at once, fine as the chaff on the threshing floor in summer, and the wind blew them away without leaving a trace. But the stone that struck the statue became a great mountain and filled the whole earth.

"This was the dream; the interpretation we shall also give in the king's presence. You, O king, are the king of kings; to you the God of heaven has given dominion and strength, power and glory; human beings, wild beasts, and birds of the air, wherever they may dwell, he has handed over to you, making you ruler over them all; you are the head of gold. Another kingdom shall take your place, inferior to yours, then a third kingdom, of bronze, which shall rule over the whole earth. There shall be a fourth kingdom, strong as iron; it shall break in pieces and subdue all these others, just as iron breaks in pieces and crushes everything else. The feet and toes you saw, partly of clay and partly of iron, mean that it shall be a divided kingdom, but yet have some of the hardness of iron. As you saw the iron mixed with clay tile, and the toes partly iron and partly clay, the kingdom shall be partly strong and partly fragile. The iron mixed with clay means that they shall seal their alliances

98

by intermarriage, but they shall not stay united, any more than iron mixes with clay. In the lifetime of those kings the God of heaven will set up a kingdom that shall never be destroyed or delivered up to another people; rather, it shall break in pieces all these kingdoms and put an end to them, and it shall stand forever. That is the meaning of the stone you saw hewn from the mountain without a hand being put to it, which broke in pieces the iron, bronze, clay, silver, and gold. The great God has revealed to the king what shall be in the future; this is exactly what you dreamed, and its meaning is sure."

In short, God gave a vision to the king of Babylon of the events leading up to the coming of the Savior and the establishment of God's Kingdom. It describes four kingdoms; 1) the Babylonian, 2) the Medal-Persian Empire, 3) the Empire of the Greeks, and finally 4) the Roman Empire. The vision shows a small stone (Jesus) coming from the heavens hitting the feet of the statue (the Roman Empire) and then that stone growing into a great mountain that fills the entire earth. The prophet describes that mountain as God's Kingdom that will last forever. Notice "the Kingdom" fills the earth (that is, it is not just heavenly).

The timing of this points to the time of Jesus. Jesus speaks of the Kingdom of God being at hand, so where is the Kingdom? We'll examine that in our next reflection.

2) Who taught that the Kingdom of Heaven is manifested on earth through His holy Church. (P)

In the remainder of this chapter I will be trying to prove this point. Getting back to our last reflection, particularly the prophecy of Daniel; we saw a "small stone" that then grew to a great mountain which

Daniel describes as God's Kingdom. The "small stone" would be Jesus who is one with His Church (the Kingdom).

It is important to understand that the phrases "the Kingdom of heaven" and "the Kingdom of God" are interchangeable. Mathew's gospel usually uses the phrase "the Kingdom of heaven" because it was written for a Jewish audience and they did not ever use the holy name of God. Mark and Luke, on the other hand, that were written for Gentile audiences, usually use the phrase "the Kingdom of God." They are not speaking of a different kingdom but are simply using language that the Gentiles were more comfortable with.

There was a biblical scholar in the late 18th century who said, "Jesus promised us the Kingdom, but all we got was the church." But as we examine the NT, especially the parables of Jesus, we will see that the "fullness of the Kingdom" will be in heaven itself, but that the Kingdom is here now present in His holy Church. We will examine this claim more thoroughly in the upcoming reflections

3) Who said the Kingdom is like a man who planted good seed, but an enemy comes and plants weeds.

Let's take a look at this parable from Mt 13:24-30

> *He proposed another parable to them. "The kingdom of heaven may be likened to a man who sowed good seed in his field. While everyone was asleep his enemy came and sowed weeds all through the wheat, and then went off. When the crop grew and bore fruit, the weeds appeared as well. The slaves of the householder came to him and said, 'Master, did you not sow good seed in your field? Where have the weeds come from?' He answered, 'An enemy has done this.' His slaves said to him,*

100

'Do you want us to go and pull them up?' He replied, 'No, if you pull up the weeds you might uproot the wheat along with them. Let them grow together until harvest; then at harvest time I will say to the harvesters, "First collect the weeds and tie them in bundles for burning; but gather the wheat into my barn."

This parable makes it clear that the Kingdom Jesus is speaking of is on earth, since there are no weeds in heaven. So when we see the Kingdom on earth (the Church) we should not be surprised to see people who we might believe look a lot like weeds rather than wheat. Jesus told us the Kingdom on earth would have weeds. We should not be surprised that some people who appear to be weeds make it to high office in the Church. After all Judas was an Apostle chosen by Jesus Himself.

It is also important to see here that the weeds will be gathered and burned at the end while the wheat will be brought into the Master's barn. The Master's barn is a reference to heaven while the burning is a reference to hell. Later in Matthew's gospel (Mt 13:41-42) Jesus says how His angles will "take out of the Kingdom" those who are evildoers and who cause others to sin and they will be thrown into "the fiery furnace." This parable, contrary to the belief of some Christians who teach that we are saved by faith alone and who believe in "the assurance of salvation" (a false doctrine that basically says that once you accept Jesus as your Lord and Savior that you are saved and nothing you do could ever undo that salvation), teaches that there are some in the visible bounds of the Church who will be judged by God to have been weeds, who will be lost for all eternity.

4) Who taught that the Kingdom of God is like a fisherman who caught all kinds of fish, good as well as bad.

Consider this parable which also appears in Mt 13:47-50

> *Again, the kingdom of heaven is like a net thrown into the sea, which collects fish of every kind. When it is full they haul it ashore and sit down to put what is good into buckets. What is bad they throw away. Thus it will be at the end of the age. The angels will go out and separate the wicked from the righteous and throw them into the fiery furnace, where there will be wailing and grinding of teeth.*

Notice again this is "the Kingdom of heaven." This is basically the same message as the previous parable: that there will be good and bad in the Kingdom here on earth. This is especially powerful when we consider that the fish was a symbol of Christians in the 1st century Church. At the end the angels will separate the good from the bad. The good will be brought to heaven and the bad will be "thrown into the fiery furnace"—a reference to hell. It is so important to notice that Jesus does not say, "When you see bad fish, then you better stay out of the Kingdom and have nothing to do with those people." Nor did He say, "When you see weeds, that means the Kingdom is no good and you are justified getting out of the Kingdom." No, Jesus tells us the good and the bad will coexist. It is not our job to judge "the bad." We are not to pull away from the Kingdom when we see "the bad." God and the angels will take care of that.

At the danger of being redundant, this parable also makes it clear that the notion of an "assurance of salvation" is very contrary to the teaching of Jesus. There are people in the visible bounds of the Church who will be lost for all eternity. This parable makes it abundantly clear that when Jesus speaks of "the Kingdom of heaven" or "the Kingdom of God" that He is usually speaking of the Church on earth. After all there are no "bad fish" in heaven as there are no "weeds" in heaven itself.

5) Who said the Kingdom of heaven is like a merchant in search of fine pearls. When he finds the pearl of great price he sells everything else and buys that one pearl.

There are actually two parables in Matthew 13 that basically have the same theme. Here are both:

> *"The kingdom of heaven is like a treasure buried in a field, which a person finds and hides again, and out of joy goes and sells all that he has and buys that field. Again, the kingdom of heaven is like a merchant searching for fine pearls. When he finds a pearl of great price, he goes and sells all that he has and buys it.*

Both parables speak of finding something of incredible value and selling everything else so that the person can have the treasure or the pearl. This tells us that the "Kingdom" is of incredible value. Which means the Church on earth is of incredible value. The Church is worth sacrificing everything. Most Christians do not feel that way about the Church these days, but that is what Jesus taught.

How has this been lived out in the history of God's people? The fact is there have been people throughout the centuries down to the present day who have sacrificed everything to build up the Church. In religious orders men and women have taken vows of poverty, chastity and obedience to serve God and build up His Kingdom here on earth—His holy Catholic Church. In doing so they and Jesus' Church have literally transformed the world. I would recommend that you read

103

David Bentley Hart's *Atheist Delusions: The Christian Revolution and Its Fashionable Enemies* to understand this better.

Basically, Hart points out how Religious men and women started the whole hospital system, they brought education to the masses, and they began the University system. Men and women who did not have their own families, who banded together to serve the Lord by serving others, and thereby transformed the world. Most people in the Western world have been fed a false history that portrays the Church as the enemy of science and freedom, but nothing could be further from the truth! Men and women who sacrificed everything for the Kingdom of God in their vows of poverty, chastity and obedience ministered to the poorest of the poor, educating them. They ministered to the sick, which was the beginning of hospitals, and they sought greater knowledge which was the beginning of universities.

Throughout the centuries tens of thousands of men and women have seen God's Kingdom as the buried treasure or the "pearl of great price" and their ministry changed everything. It is tragic that so few of our young men and women today see God's Kingdom as such a great treasure and never consider serving God and His Kingdom as a priest, brother, sister or deacon. Only in the Catholic Church have we seen men and women willing to abandon everything worldly to serve the Lord.

6) Who taught that the Kingdom is like a king who threw a wedding banquet for his son.

Look at this parable from the 22nd chapter of Matthew:1-14:

> *Jesus again in reply spoke to them in parables, saying, "The kingdom of heaven may be likened to a king who gave a*

wedding feast for his son. He dispatched his servants to summon the invited guests to the feast, but they refused to come. A second time he sent other servants, saying, 'Tell those invited: "Behold, I have prepared my banquet, my calves and fattened cattle are killed, and everything is ready; come to the feast."' Some ignored the invitation and went away, one to his farm, another to his business. The rest laid hold of his servants, mistreated them, and killed them. The king was enraged and sent his troops, destroyed those murderers, and burned their city. Then he said to his servants, 'The feast is ready, but those who were invited were not worthy to come. Go out, therefore, into the main roads and invite to the feast whomever you find.' The servants went out into the streets and gathered all they found, bad and good alike, and the hall was filled with guests. But when the king came in to meet the guests he saw a man there not dressed in a wedding garment. He said to him, 'My friend, how is it that you came in here without a wedding garment?' But he was reduced to silence. Then the king said to his attendants, 'Bind his hands and feet, and cast him into the darkness outside, where there will be wailing and grinding of teeth.' Many are invited, but few are chosen."

This parable has a twofold purpose. The first purpose was aimed at Jesus' immediate listeners. Jesus says that the king was enraged and sent his troops to destroy those murderers and to burn their city. This is clearly a reference to those in Jesus' day who rejected Him. God gave the people of Jerusalem the typical biblical 40 years to come to faith and when they refused the city of Jerusalem was destroyed. Jesus speaks elsewhere about the Temple and how not one stone will be left on another (see Mt 24:1-14).

But this parable also has a meaning for all subsequent generations of Christians. We see in the Book of Revelation how the Mass is described as the "wedding banquet of the Lamb" (see Scott Hahn's book, *The Lamb's Supper*). Jesus invites all people to this banquet, but sadly many refuse to come. The excuses we hear for people not attending Mass are as flimsy as those who do not come to the wedding feast in this parable. Just as it was utter foolishness of the people of Jerusalem to not put their faith in Jesus; today it is utter foolishness when the Savior of the world offers us His own body and blood and some stay away.

7) Who taught that in the Kingdom of God our receiving of forgiveness is related to our giving of forgiveness.

When Jesus taught us to pray the Lord's Prayer in Mt 6 He included the petition that we should be forgiven as we have forgiven others. When He finishes teaching us that beautiful prayer He follows it up by saying in verses 14-15 *"If you forgive others their transgressions, your heavenly Father will forgive you. But if you do not forgive others, neither will your Father forgive your transgressions."*

Jesus also presents a parable teaching this in Mt 18:21-25:

> *Then Peter approaching asked him, "Lord, if my brother sins against me, how often must I forgive him? As many as seven times?" Jesus answered, "I say to you, not seven times but seventy-seven times. That is why the kingdom of heaven may be likened to a king who decided to settle accounts with his servants. When he began the accounting, a debtor was brought before him who owed him a huge amount. Since he had no way of paying it back, his master ordered him to be sold, along with his wife, his children, and all his property, in payment of the*

debt. At that, the servant fell down, did him homage, and said, 'Be patient with me, and I will pay you back in full.' Moved with compassion the master of that servant let him go and forgave him the loan. When that servant had left, he found one of his fellow servants who owed him a much smaller amount. He seized him and started to choke him, demanding, 'Pay back what you owe.' Falling to his knees, his fellow servant begged him, 'Be patient with me, and I will pay you back.' But he refused. Instead, he had him put in prison until he paid back the debt. Now when his fellow servants saw what had happened, they were deeply disturbed, and went to their master and reported the whole affair. His master summoned him and said to him, 'You wicked servant! I forgave you your entire debt because you begged me to. Should you not have had pity on your fellow servant, as I had pity on you?' Then in anger his master handed him over to the torturers until he should pay back the whole debt. So will my heavenly Father do to you, unless each of you forgives his brother from his heart."

Jesus makes it very clear that if we want His forgiveness we need to forgive one another. I ask you to consider this teaching in light of the belief of many Christians that we are saved by "faith alone." Obviously Jesus is teaching us that our actions have a huge impact on our salvation. Without forgiveness we cannot make it to heaven and Jesus is clear that forgiving others is required if we are to receive His forgiveness.

However, at the end of the parable Jesus speaks of the person being released from "the torturers." It is important to make a distinction between temporary punishment and eternal punishment. Jesus here seems to be indicating a place of temporary punishment. That would imply what we Catholics refer to as "purgatory." What if a person has

107

not completely forgiven those who have offended him or her, but they go to confession and receive the absolution of the Church; are they still not forgiven? The answer is that they are forgiven, but they will need more purification in purgatory since they have not found it in their heart to forgive their neighbor. We see in this God's incredible mercy. Even though He desperately wants us to forgive one another; when we find that difficult to do we can still be saved but will need purification before we enter into the glory of heaven.

8) Who said to Simon, son of Jonah, "You are rock and on this rock I will build my church."

Here we are examining Mt 16:13-19 which is the basis of this reflection and the next:

> When Jesus went into the region of Caesarea Philippi he asked his disciples, "Who do people say that the Son of Man is?" They replied, "Some say John the Baptist, others Elijah, still others Jeremiah or one of the prophets." He said to them, "But who do you say that I am?" Simon Peter said in reply, "You are the Messiah, the Son of the living God." Jesus said to him in reply, "Blessed are you, Simon son of Jonah. For flesh and blood has not revealed this to you, but my heavenly Father. And so I say to you, you are Peter, and upon this rock I will build my church, and the gates of the netherworld shall not prevail against it. I will give you the keys to the kingdom of heaven. Whatever you bind on earth shall be bound in heaven; and whatever you loose on earth shall be loosed in heaven

In this passage Jesus asks the Apostles who He is, and as so often happens, the man Jesus is about to rename answers, that is Peter. So

Peter tells Jesus who He is, then Jesus turns around and tells Peter who he is, giving him a new name.

Some translations say, "You are Peter and on this rock I will build my church" and others translate it, "You are Rock and on this rock I will build my church." Why the difference? It has to do with the way names are translated. Some translators choose to translate a name using what is called "transliteration". Transliteration is when you make a name from one language sound like a word in the language you are translating into. The above translation is a transliteration which takes the Greek word "petros" and makes it sound English-"Peter". Other translators take the meaning of the word in the original language and translate it into a comparable word in a new language. A strict translation of Mat16:16 would be "You are rock and on this rock, I will build my church." Personally, I prefer the "translation" to the "transliteration," but the New American Bible which we use at Mass uses the "transliteration."

There are many who try to explain away the renaming of Peter arguing that "petros" really means "little stone" and that Jesus is contrasting Peter with Himself who is the true "rock." In the original Greek we have, "you are "petros" and on this "petra" I will build my church." There is a slight difference in the two words which many use as a reason to deny that Peter is actually the rock on whom Jesus will build His Church. How are we to understand this?

The Greek language, like Spanish or Italian, have word endings that are masculine or feminine. The word in Greek for "rock" is a feminine word, "petra." In giving this name to a man, the word had to be masculinized rendering his name "Petros." When people try to explain away the significance of Peter's name they sound reasonable until we examine the scriptures more deeply. We see throughout the NT the

109

name of Peter translated both in a translation and in a transliteration. For instance in John 1:42 we read, "Then he brought him to Jesus. Jesus looked at him and said, 'you are Simon son of John; you will be called Cephas' which is translated Peter." We also see St. Paul on eight different occasions refer to Peter as Cephas; 1Cor1:12, 3:22, 9:5, 15:5, Gal1:18, 2:9, 2:11, and 2:14. What is the significance of this? From this rendering of Peter's name we can see what Jesus actually said, since He spoke Aramaic and not Greek. What Jesus actually said was, "you are cepha and on this cepha I will build my church." It was the same word in both places. "Cephas" is the transliteration of the Aramaic word for "rock,"-cepha.

The biggest problem with the rendering in the New American translation, of course, is that "Peter" and "rock" look nothing alike. A casual reader would have no clue to the true meaning of Peter's name. As we search the Scriptures we see that whenever God gave someone a new name it implied that they were to have a key role in salvation history. That, of course, is true of Peter who Jesus made the leader of the Apostles. But does the fact that Jesus renamed Peter have significance when it comes to the issue of authority? We will examine that issue in our next reflection.

9) **Who said to Simon Peter, "I will give you the keys of the kingdom of heaven. Whatever you bind on earth I will hold bound in heaven. Whatever you loose on earth, shall be loosed in heaven."**

There are many outside the Catholic Church who believe Jesus did this so we could tell jokes about Peter meeting us at the gates of heaven when we die. But that, of course, is not what Jesus intended. Jesus here is reaching back to the OT and using an image that would have been very familiar to His Jewish listeners. His Jewish listeners would have clearly understood that Jesus was referring to a symbol for an OT office in the kingdom of David. Let's take a look at Is 22:15-22

> *"Thus says the Lord, the GOD of hosts: Up, go to that official, Shebna, master of the palace, "What have you here? Whom have you here, that you have hewn for yourself a tomb here, Hewing a tomb on high, carving a resting place in the rock?" The LORD shall hurl you down headlong, mortal man!*

> *He shall grip you firmly, And roll you up and toss you like a ball into a broad land. There you will die, there with the chariots you glory in, you disgrace to your master's house! I will thrust you from your office and pull you down from your station. On that day I will summon my servant Eliakim, son of Hilkiah, I will clothe him with your robe, gird him with your sash, confer on him your authority.*

> ***He shall be a father to the inhabitants of Jerusalem***, *and to the house of Judah.* ***I will place the key of the House of David on his shoulder; what he opens, no one will shut, what he shuts, no one will open"*** (emphasis mine).

Here we see two men, Shebna and Eliakim. Shebna is "the master of the palace." What does that mean? Well he was (in today's terms) the prime minister of one of the kings in the line of David. But Shebna lost the favor of the Lord and was to be removed from his office and replaced with Eliakim. It is essential to see here that the symbol of this prestigious office is "the key of the house of David." So, in Matthew 16 we see Jesus who is a king in the line of David giving "the keys of the Kingdom" to Peter. In this He is establishing an office for His Kingdom on earth, His holy Church. Notice in verse 20 that Eliakim, the new prime minister, will be a "father" to the people of God. It is

111

also important to take note that this event in Isaiah is roughly 500 years after the time of King David. In other words, there is succession with the one who has the "key of the house of David." In the OT kingdom of David, the kings died and a new king took his place, but the prime ministers also had successors. In the NT the King is always the same (Jesus), but His prime minister continues to change with the passing of time. So, while Jesus gave the "keys" to Peter, the symbol implies an office with a successor. The successor is the Bishop of Rome whom we call "the pope." The word "pope" comes from the Italian "papa" which means "father." So just as Eliakim was to be a father to God's OT people, the one with the "keys" today is a father to God's NT people. This is why we call the pope "the Holy Father."

This is the biblical way to understand what Jesus was doing in Matthew 16:13-19. Unfortunately, many people today refuse to submit to the one with this God-given authority. However, we have already seen in the first section of this book how Jesus Himself was obedient to legitimate human authority. Jesus, who is God, obeyed Joseph and Mary, mere humans. If God Himself chose to obey legitimate human authority, how can any Christian refuse to obey the legitimate authority of the one who holds the keys of the Kingdom today? We will examine the issue of authority more fully in the last section of this book.

10) Who taught that the Kingdom of heaven is manifested on earth through His holy Church. (P)

We end this chapter as we began, that the "Kingdom" Jesus speaks of is His holy Church on earth. To be sure, the fulfillment of the Kingdom will be in heaven itself, but to ignore the Church on earth is to reject God's Kingdom and God's plan. Jesus is not going to come after some imaginary "rapture" to establish His Kingdom. He established that Kingdom 2,000 years ago. He established officers and granted them His own authority. Jesus warns us in Mt 12:25ff of the dangers of a divided Kingdom. He says a kingdom divided will not stand. The divisions that are rampant in His Church are certainly not the Will of God. We will examine that issue of authority much more fully in the last section of the book, but it is so important that we realize that the Church is not some incidental aspect of God's plan of salvation. In fact in several passages it speaks of Jesus proclaiming "the gospel of the kingdom" (see Mt 4:23 and 24:14) In other words, the gospel is all about the Kingdom; it is all about the Church.

Holy Mary, Mother of God, pray for us sinners
now and at the hour of our death. Amen.

Glory be to the Father,
and to the Son, and to the Holy Spirit:
As it was in the beginning,
is now, and ever shall be, world without end. Amen

Oh my Jesus, forgive us our sins, save us from the power of hell.
Lead all souls to heaven, especially those
most in need of your mercy, amen.

113

The Fourth Luminous Mystery
The Transfiguration

Hail Mary, full of grace, the Lord is with you; blessed are you among women, and blessed is the fruit of your womb, **Jesus:**

1) Who wanted to demonstrate that the law and the prophets were pointing to Him and were fulfilled by Him. (P)

The whole Bible is about Jesus. The books of the OT were often referred to as "the law and the prophets." The giver of the law was Moses. The proto-typical prophet was Elijah. In appearing with the two of them Jesus was demonstrating that the whole OT was pointing to His saving work. The whole OT was getting ready for all that Jesus would do. But to understand how the OT pointed us to the Lord we need to understand OT "types". A "type" is a person, place or thing in the OT that points us to a person, place or thing in the NT. "Typology" is really at the heart of understanding how the OT prepared the world for the coming of Jesus. In the OT there are several types of Jesus. But there are also types of Mary; types of baptism; types of the holy Eucharist; types of the Church and types for the pope. Earlier we spoke of how the prime minister in the kingdom of David was getting us ready for the papacy and was the foundation for understanding Matthew 16. As we go forward we will see many more "types" that were getting us ready for all that Jesus would accomplish. So the "law and the prophets" were pointing us to Jesus, but Jesus also fulfills the "law and the prophets." The beginning and the end of the Bible is Jesus. That is the basic message of the Transfiguration.

2) Who wanted to give the Apostles a glimpse of His glory before He entered into His Passion.

While Jesus had to fulfill the OT He was also very aware of the very ordinary men He had called to be Apostles. They were going to see the One they had left everything for, be arrested, beaten, mocked, scourged and crucified. He needed to shore them up with an amazing demonstration of who He really was. So He allowed the Apostles to see Him with the two who best represented the OT. This would strengthen them at their lowest hours when Jesus was crucified. The memory of the Transfiguration had to give the Apostles hope when all seemed lost.

3) Who took Peter, James and John to a high mountain to pray with them.

One of the important things to understand as we look at how Jesus fulfilled the expectations of the OT, is to see what exactly those expectations were. Dr. Brandt Pitre in his book, *The Jewish roots of the Eucharist* explains that God's people were expecting a new Moses, a new Passover, a new Exodus, and of course a new Covenant. The NT portrays Jesus as the new Moses. We see that in Matthew's gospel with several parallels in the life of Moses with the life of Jesus. When Moses was born the king of Egypt was trying to kill all the male Israelite boys. When Jesus is born, wicked king Herod has all the young boys of Bethlehem slaughtered. Moses comes up out of Egypt, Jesus' parents take Him to Egypt to save Him from Herod, but then Jesus comes out of Egypt and returns to Judah. Moses gives us the commandments from a mountain; Jesus gives us the new commandments in the "sermon on the mount." Matthew goes to great lengths to show that Jesus is the new Moses.

In the Transfiguration we see Jesus again portrayed as the new Moses. We see Jesus take three of His closest Apostles with Him up the mountain. In Exodus 24:1 we see Moses go up the mountain with

115

Aaron, Nadab and Abihu (Nadab and Abihu were Aaron's sons). These three formed a special core around Moses as Peter, James and John were a special core around Jesus. One of the expectations of the Jews was "a prophet like unto Moses" (Deut. 18:15 & Acts 3:22). The Transfiguration is one more parallel between Moses and Jesus.

4) Whose clothes became dazzling white; whiter than is humanly possible.

Consider Matthew's description of the Transfiguration which is found in the 17th chapter of his gospel which we will focus on throughout this chapter, verses 1-9:

> *After six days Jesus took Peter, James, and John his brother, and led them up a high mountain by themselves. And he was transfigured before them; his face shone like the sun and his clothes became white as light. And behold, Moses and Elijah appeared to them, conversing with him. Then Peter said to Jesus in reply, "Lord, it is good that we are here. If you wish, I will make three tents here, one for you, one for Moses, and one for Elijah." While he was still speaking, behold, a bright cloud cast a shadow over them, then from the cloud came a voice that said, "This is my beloved Son, with whom I am well pleased; listen to Him." When the disciples heard this, they fell prostrate and were very much afraid. But Jesus came and touched them, saying, "Rise, and do not be afraid." And when the disciples raised their eyes, they saw no one else but Jesus alone.*

> *As they were coming down from the mountain, Jesus charged them, "Do not tell the vision to anyone until the Son of Man has been raised from the dead."*

The gospel writer makes it clear that this was no ordinary event. Jesus is clothed in glory for His Apostles to see.

5) Whose face radiated the very glory of God.

I've already explained how the Jewish people were expecting a new Moses. This is one more similarity between Jesus and Moses. We see in Exodus 34:29-35 that Moses face became radiant when he encountered the Lord.

> *As Moses came down from Mount Sinai with the two tablets of the covenant in his hands, he did not know that the skin of his face had become radiant while he spoke with the LORD. When Aaron, then, and the other Israelites saw Moses and noticed how radiant the skin of his face had become, they were afraid to come near him. Only after Moses called to them did Aaron and all the leaders of the community come back to him. Moses then spoke to them. Later, all the Israelites came up to him, and he enjoined on them all that the LORD had told him on Mount Sinai. When Moses finished speaking with them, he put a veil over his face. Whenever Moses entered the presence of the LORD to speak with him, he removed the veil until he came out again. On coming out, he would tell the Israelites all that he had been commanded. Then the Israelites would see that the skin of Moses' face was radiant; so he would again put the veil over his face until he went in to speak with the LORD.*

In the transfiguration we see Jesus once again portrayed as the new Moses. As Moses' face became radiant when he encountered the Lord, Jesus' face now radiates the very glory of God.

117

6) Who appeared with Moses, the giver of the law.

7) Who appeared with Elijah, the greatest of the prophets.

As I mentioned already the whole OT was often referred to as the "law and the prophets." In appearing with Moses, the giver of the law and Elijah the proto-typical prophet, Jesus intends to teach us that the whole OT was pointing to Him and was fulfilled by Him.

8) Who spoke to Moses and Elijah about His upcoming exodus that was to take place in Jerusalem.

We need to look at Luke's description of the Transfiguration to see this important point. In Luke 9:31 we see that Jesus spoke to Moses and Elijah about His upcoming exodus. This is to fulfill the expectations of the Jewish people that there would be a new exodus.

In the original exodus God's people went from a life of slavery to a new life of freedom. In the saving work of Jesus we are delivered from our slavery to sin to a new life of freedom from sin. In this Jesus is pointing us to a new exodus and the fact that He is the new Moses.

9) Who said to the Apostles, "Tell no one of the vision until the Son of Man has risen from the dead."

We need to turn to Mark's gospel to see this instruction of the Lord to the Apostles as they were coming down the mountain. As we see in Mark chapter 9 Jesus gives the Apostles specific instructions to tell no one of the vision until the Son of Man has risen from the dead. Let's take a look at that passage, verses 9-11:

"As they were coming down from the mountain, he charged them not to relate what they had seen to anyone, except when the Son of Man had risen from the dead. So they kept the matter to themselves, questioning what rising from the dead meant."

You have to love the Apostles! Even at this point they are somewhat clueless as to what all of this means. It fills me with such great hope when I see them struggle to understand, because I so often struggle with sin and ignorance. If these men who had spent three years with Jesus sometimes struggled to understand and yet we refer to them as "saints," it gives me hope that despite my weaknesses and failings that I might someday become a saint.

10) Who wanted to demonstrate that the law and the prophets were pointing to Him and fulfilled by Him. (P)

We finish where we began, that the point of the Transfiguration was teaching us that the whole Bible was pointing us to Jesus.

Holy Mary, Mother of God, pray for us sinners
now and at the hour of our death. Amen.

Glory be to the Father,
and to the Son, and to the Holy Spirit:
As it was in the beginning,
is now, and ever shall be, world without end. Amen

Oh my Jesus, forgive our sins and save us from the power of hell.
Lead all souls into heaven especially those
most in need of your mercy. Amen

The Fifth Luminous Mystery
The Last Supper

Hail Mary, full of grace, the Lord is with you; blessed are you among women, and blessed is the fruit of your womb, ***Jesus:***

1) Who gave us His own Body and Blood at the Last Supper. (P)

You will notice that this reflection is not only in bold, but is in larger font as well. That is because this is the most awesome mystery of our faith. The fact is that our God shares His very life with us every time we receive Holy Communion. This is the pinnacle of God's plan of salvation.

To understand the Eucharist, we need to once again go back to Genesis. At the beginning there was a forbidden food. God said to our first parents, "Don't eat this or you will die." Our first parents of course ate the forbidden food and with that brought sin and death into the world. Now in saving us God gives us a commanded food. Let's take a look at what Jesus said about the Eucharist in the 6th chapter of St. John's gospel, verses 48-71:

> *I am the bread of life. Your ancestors ate the manna in the desert, but they died; this is the bread that comes down from heaven so that one may eat it and not die. I am the living bread that came down from heaven; whoever eats this bread will live forever; and the bread that I will give is my flesh for the life of the world."*

The Jews quarreled among themselves, saying, "How can this man give us [his] flesh to eat?" Jesus said to them, "Amen, amen, I say to you, unless you eat the flesh of the Son of Man and drink his blood, you do not have life within you. Whoever eats my flesh and drinks my blood has eternal life, and I will raise him on the last day. For my flesh is true food, and my blood is true drink. Whoever eats my flesh and drinks my blood remains in me and I in him. Just as the living Father sent me and I have life because of the Father, so also the one who feeds on me will have life because of me. This is the bread that came down from heaven. Unlike your ancestors who ate and still died, whoever eats this bread will live forever." These things he said while teaching in the synagogue in Capernaum.

Then many of his disciples who were listening said, "This saying is hard; who can accept it?" Since Jesus knew that his disciples were murmuring about this, he said to them, "Does this shock you? What if you were to see the Son of Man ascending to where he was before - It is the spirit that gives life, while the flesh is of no avail. The words I have spoken to you are spirit and life. But there are some of you who do not believe." Jesus knew from the beginning the ones who would not believe and the one who would betray Him. And he said, "For this reason I have told you that no one can come to me unless it is granted him by my Father."

As a result of this, many [of] His disciples returned to their former way of life and no longer accompanied Him. Jesus then said to the Twelve, "Do you also want to leave?" Simon Peter answered Him, "Master, to whom shall we go? You have the words of eternal life. We have come to believe and are convinced that You are the Holy One of God." Jesus answered them, "Did I not choose you twelve? Yet is not one of you a devil?" He was referring to Judas, son of Simon the Iscariot; it was he who would betray Him, one of the Twelve.

Jesus in verse 53 says, "Amen, amen"—that is an oath formula; Jesus is literally saying, "I swear to you if you don't eat my body and drink my blood you have no life in you." In the gospels of Matthew, Mark and Luke as well as in First Corinthians we are told how Jesus gave us the Holy Eucharist at the Last Supper and commanded the Apostles, "Do this in remembrance of me." The "Do this" is in the imperative sense in the Greek—that is, this is an urgent command. And yet there are literally millions of followers of Christ who Sunday after Sunday refuse to obey the command of the Lord. As our first parents foolishly ate the forbidden food, there are millions who foolishly refuse to eat the commanded food.

It's also important to recognize that in the Fall and our salvation there is a mirror image. You know as you look in a mirror and you raise your left hand; the right hand of the image goes up. There is the same kind of dynamic between the Fall and our salvation. At the Fall the food looked good, it smelled good, it seemed desirable. Adam and Eve could have felt, "what's the difference, it can't be too bad, it smells great." In salvation we have the mirror image in that the commanded food looks very ordinary, it does not look or smell special; so many today feel, "It can't be anything special because it looks so ordinary." But the bottom line in all of this is when God tells you not to eat something then you shouldn't eat it. When God tells you that you must do something, it's a good idea to do it!

In the story of creation there are two trees mentioned specifically by name. The "forbidden fruit" which was the tree of the knowledge of good and evil and there was also "the tree of life." Why was there a

122

tree of life in the garden? After all, Adam and Eve were not supposed to die; death only came into the world as a result of sin.

This gets us to the nature of the test that God gave our first parents which will help us understand why Jesus did what He did. In Hebrews 2:15 we are told that is was through "the fear of death" that our first parents fell. Most of us have an image of the Fall that Adam and Eve were tricked by a little snake, but the Greek translation of the OT uses the same word in Genesis that is used in the Book of Revelation to describe the seven-headed dragon. That is what we should picture in the Garden. And of course, Adam was the one God put in charge of guarding the Garden, so if a seven-headed dragon got in, who let him in? Adam did! What Adam was supposed to do was go to the "tree of life" and eat its fruit then stand between the dragon and his bride to protect her, but he failed miserably! Now in all honesty, the dragon probably would have killed Adam and then God would have raised him up (had Adam eaten the fruit of "the tree of life"). But it appears that Adam stood back and basically said to his bride, "you talk to the dragon, Honey!" After the woman eats the forbidden fruit she gives it to Adam to eat, so he was there!

This gives us insight into what Jesus did for our salvation. Our first parents sinned at a tree, so Jesus is "hung on a tree" (see Acts 35:30 &10:39). Adam did not go to the "the tree of life," but the earliest Christians referred to the Eucharist as, "the fruit of the tree of life."

When we look at Genesis we see that sin separated us not only from God, but from one another as well. Sin divides us. We see this when Adam says, "**the woman you** put here." Adam basically made excuses for his sin by blaming the woman and even God Himself (you put her here God!). We see the same message reinforced in Genesis 11 with the story of the Tower of Babel. At that point the whole world speaks one language, but because of sin they are divided into nations and cultures that do not understand each other and often don't like each other. The message is sin divides us.

So, the pinnacle of God's plan is the Holy Eucharist. Whenever we receive "Holy Communion" we are united to God and to one another. In Communion we are made one in Jesus. This is what Jesus came to do; this is the high point of all of salvation history. This is the be all and end all of faith, or as the Second Vatican Council called it, "the source and summit" of faith. It's the source because the Eucharist is Jesus Himself the source of all we have and are. It's the summit for the same reason, Jesus is the goal of life.

As we continue through this chapter we will see that God actually gave us two gifts to keep us united. He gave us the Holy Eucharist, but He also gave Divine authority to human beings so that we could remain united. We will deal much more thoroughly with the issue of authority in the last section of this book, but in this section, we will examine the establishment of the NT priesthood.

2) Who said to the Apostles that He earnestly desired to eat this Passover with them.

The phrase "earnestly desired" comes from the Revised Standard translation of the Bible. It implies a deep desire, a yearning, a longing to eat this meal with them. The question is why? For many Christians the Last Supper was a meal that we think back fondly upon, but it had no salvific value. In their minds we do it because Jesus told us to do it, but it is merely a ritual. But that would not explain why Jesus earnestly desired to eat this particular meal. If there was no salvific action at the meal Jesus could have just as easily as said, "These last days or weeks have been precious to me" or "It's always meant so much to me when we can share a meal together" or "We're really getting close to my saving actions now," but that's not what He said. He said He earnestly desired to eat this meal, why?

First, the expectation of the Jewish people was for a "new Passover." Remember the original Passover was not just a ritual, those who participated in it were saved from death. The Israelites in Exodus were saved by "the blood of the lamb," but to be saved by the blood they had to eat the lamb (see Exodus 12:1-13, especially verses 7-11). The Passover was a perpetual institution among the Israelites and the Jewish people expected a "new Passover" to be instituted by the Messiah.

Second, as we will see throughout this section, Jesus' greatest desire was for His disciples to be one. At the Last Supper Jesus will give us the two gifts intended to keep us united, the Holy Eucharist and priestly authority. This meal was not an empty ritual that we are to think back on fondly, it was to be an integral part of the saving work of the Lord.

3) Who ordained the Apostles priests of the new covenant through the prayers and the washing of the feet.

Since there are many Christians who deny that Jesus established a ministerial priesthood, we'll need to examine the biblical evidence for a NT ministerial priesthood. For the most part all Christians (including Catholics) believe in the common priesthood of the faithful. This was also part of the OT. We see in Exodus 19:6 that God was making the Israelites into a kingdom of priests; and yet there was still a ministerial priesthood from the tribe of Levi. In the NT Jesus makes all His faithful people share in His priesthood, but we also see Him establish a ministerial priesthood at the Last Supper. To deny the ministerial priesthood requires one to ignore the teaching of the Bible.

Let's examine the promises of the OT. In Isaiah 66 the prophet foresees the day when the Lord will gather people of all nations and languages into His covenant family. And Isaiah says, *"Some of these I will take as priests and Levites says the Lord"* (Isaiah 66:21). Now since Jesus established the new and eternal covenant, there is no way this promise of scripture could ever be fulfilled unless Jesus established a ministerial priesthood. After all, as Christians we believe that all believers share in the common priesthood; so the promise, **"some of them** I will make priests..." does not match up with the reality if there is not a ministerial priesthood. As Catholics we believe all believers share the common priesthood, but that God calls certain men to the ministerial priesthood. That certainly matches the promise of Isaiah.

If we look at Jude 11 we see this very interesting line: *Woe to them! They followed the way of Cain, abandoned themselves to Balam's error for the sake of gain, and perished in the rebellion of Korah.* In context, it is very clear that Jude is speaking of Christians who are a part of the Christian community who have fallen into these sins, but we need to look at the OT to understand what he is referring to. What we need to focus on is the phrase, "...and perished in the rebellion of Korah." What was the rebellion of Korah? If we look at Numbers 16 through Numbers 17:5 we see that it was a twofold rebellion. It was first of all a rebellion against the God-given authority of Moses; and secondly it was a rebellion against the ministerial priesthood. In Numbers this rebellion is reported along with the rebellions of Dathan and Abiram so it becomes a little confusing. The short of what happened was that Korah and 250 other Levites challenged Moses' authority because they were not to be ministerial priests. In verse 3 we

126

are told that they held an assembly against Moses; in verse 10 Moses says to Korah and his followers, *"He has allowed you and your kinsmen, the descendants of Levi to approach him, and yet you now seek the priesthood too."* We see at the end that Korah and his 250 followers are severely punished by the Lord for their rebellion. So how could people in NT times "perish in the rebellion of Korah" if there is not a NT ministerial priesthood?

How does Jesus ordain the Apostles priests at the Last Supper? To understand this, we need to once again examine the OT. In Leviticus 8:6 we see that part of the ordination rite for Aaron and his sons was that they were to be washed. Jesus washes the feet of His Apostles at the Last Supper. (see also Ex 30:19-21; Ex 40:31)

Second, there are many references to "sacrifice" at the Last Supper. Jesus speaks of a "new Covenant." Covenants were sealed in blood. When Jesus says, "This is my blood, the blood of the new and everlasting covenant that will be shed for you and for the many;" He is using sacrificial language. Since the role of the priest was to offer sacrifice and Jesus commands them "to do this in remembrance of me," it is clear that Jesus is commanding them to offer sacrifice, a priestly role. The first priest mentioned in the Bible was Melchizedek. In Genesis 14: 18-20 we read:

> *"Melchizedek, king of Salem, brought out bread and wine. He was a priest of God Most High. He blessed Abram with these words: "Blessed be Abram by God Most High, the creator of heaven and earth; And blessed be God Most High, who delivered your foes into your hand." Then Abram gave him a tenth of everything."*

So the sacrifice of the first priest in the Bible was bread and wine. Jesus is a priest in the line of Melchizedek so His sacrifice also needed to include bread and wine. Since Jesus commanded the Apostles to "do this in remembrance of me" He was empowering them to offer the same sacrifice He Himself had just offered.

Finally, in the OT one of the few places we see the word translated as "consecrate" is in the ordination of the priests (we also see it with making things that will be used in the worship of God holy). In fact the High Priest wore a headpiece that said, "Consecrated to the Lord." Jesus three times prays that the Father will consecrate the Apostles in truth (John 17:17 & 19).

4) Who prayed that His disciples would be one as He and the Father are one.

5) Who prayed that there be such perfect unity among His disciples that the world would come to believe in Him.

Perhaps you've noticed that the world today does not believe in Jesus. Even in parts of the world that historically have been Christian we see more and more unbelievers. Could it have something to do with the fact that there are so many divisions among Christians? Jesus prayed for perfect unity, but we now have roughly 38,000 churches all disagreeing with each other. There are even Christian groups that hold other Christians in great disdain; this obviously is not the Will of God!

Look at what Jesus prayed the night before He died. We find this in the 17th chapter of St. John's gospel, verses 20-23:

> *"I pray not only for them, but also for those who will believe in me through their word, so **that they may all be one,** as you,*

128

*Father, are in me and I in you, that they also may be in us, that the world may believe that you sent me. And I have given them the glory you gave me, **so that they may be one, as we are one**, I in them and you in me, **that they may be brought to perfection as one**, that the world may know that you sent me, and that you loved them even as you loved me. (emphasis mine)*

This comes from Jesus' high priestly prayer at the Last Supper. Some theologians refer to this as "Jesus' last will and testament", since He is praying what is most on His heart the night before He dies. And what is most on is heart? He prays that His disciples will be one as He and the Father are one. That is incredible unity for which He is praying. He prays that the unity of His disciples will be so perfect that the world will come to believe in Him. As we saw already there is more and more disunity among Christians corresponding with a greater and greater loss of faith in what was previously known as "Christendom." How can this be turned around?

Jesus left two things to assure our unity; the Holy Eucharist and Divine authority entrusted to human beings. We have already examined the gift of the NT priesthood. In the last section of this book we will thoroughly examine God given authority in His Church. But for now, I believe it is essential for all Christians to examine themselves. Are we humble enough to obey those with God given authority? We saw in the reflection on the finding of Jesus in the Temple as a twelve-year-old that He humbled Himself to by obedient to His earthly parents, will we be humble enough to obey those with religious authority over us?

6) Who took bread, blessed it, broke it and gave it to His disciples saying, "take this all of you and eat it, for this is my body."

129

I realize that this is wordier than, at first glance, it would appear that it needs to be, but there is a fourfold action of the Lord that is important to examine. We will see this fourfold action in several events in the ministry of Jesus that is pointing us to the Holy Eucharist. First there is the multiplication of the loaves. In Luke 9:16 we see this same fourfold action of taking, blessing, breaking and giving the bread to the crowd. The miracle of the multiplication of the loaves was meant to point us to the even greater miracle of Jesus feeding us with "bread from heaven."

At the Last Supper Jesus again takes the bread, blesses it, breaks it and then gives it. And finally, after the Resurrection when He arrives at Emmaus with two of His disciples we see this same fourfold action. Luke, in using the same words at all of these events, is attempting to help the reader see how they all go together. We will discuss the journey to Emmaus more fully in the last section of this book and how it is pointing us to the Mass. But for now, it is clear that Jesus gave us His own Body and Blood at the Last Supper.

Some people try to explain away the plain words of Jesus by arguing that the Lord was merely trying to convey that His followers must have a very intimate relationship with Him. That in speaking of eating His Body and drinking His Blood He was using an image to convey true intimacy, since food eaten is very much united to the person eating it. But this explanation ignores how "eating people" is used elsewhere in the Bible. In Micah 3:3, Psalm 14:4 and 53:5 all speak of eating people or devouring people in a figurative way; and it is described as a terrible injustice to the innocent. So to claim that Jesus was speaking figuratively that we must eat His flesh is to use the image in the exact opposite way that it is used in other biblical passages. In other words Jesus would be saying something like, "Unless you do terrible things to me you cannot have life in you."

That of course is nonsense. There are many words in Greek that the biblical authors could have used that would imply a symbolic meaning behind eating and drinking, but they did not use those words. The words of scripture imply what Catholics have believed for 2,000 years; that is, Jesus gave us His own body and blood at the Last Supper and empowered the Apostles as priests of the New Covenant to offer the same sacrifice.

7) **Who took the Chalice filled with wine and said, "This is my blood."**

8) **Who said to the Apostles, "This is the blood of the new and eternal covenant, which will be poured out for you and for many for the forgiveness of sin."**

These words of Jesus echo the words of Moses when the OT covenant was made at Mount Sinai. In Exodus 24:8 we read: *"Then he took the blood and splashed it on the people, saying, "This is the blood of the covenant which the LORD has made with you according to all these words."* In Exodus Moses sprinkled real blood on the people to seal the covenant. Jesus really gave us His blood at the Last Supper to bring about His New Covenant.

9) **Who commanded the Apostles to "Do this in remembrance of me."**

I'm told by those whom I trust that Jesus uses the imperative here, this is an urgent command. This is not some casual ritual that we can choose to participate in or choose to ignore. We choose to ignore this command at our own peril. In Genesis God told our first parents, "Don't do this" now in saving us, the same God commands us to "Do this." To ignore this command would be as foolish as Adam and Eve ignoring the command about the forbidden fruit.

The word "remembrance" is how this is translated in the Revised Standard Version of the Bible. I use that translation here because it better harkens back to the OT usage. In Exodus 2:24-25 we read (this is the Revised Standard Version translation), *And God heard their groaning, and God remembered his covenant with Abraham, with Isaac, and with Jacob. And God saw the people of Israel, and God knew their condition.* What are we to make of God's remembering His covenant? Should we picture God striking Himself in the head saying, "those are my people, I almost forgot?" Of course not! The OT meaning of the word remembrance was connected to an action that would unleash the graces of the covenant. In remembering the covenant, it implies that God will take action that showers His grace of salvation upon them.

In the same way the Israelites saw their yearly celebration of the Passover as a remembrance that made them present at the original Passover. They were not just thinking back fondly of what God had done for their ancestors; no, they themselves were present at the original event. They were participating in God's saving grace. The Passover transcended time and space and they were there even though they may have been born centuries after the original event.

In commanding the Apostles to "Do this in remembrance of me" Jesus is implying that in doing this, the graces of the covenant will be unleashed. Every time we come to Mass we are at the Last Supper, we stand with Mary at the foot of the cross, and we come to the empty tomb. In doing this action the graces that Jesus won for us on the cross are showered upon His people. At Mass we do not just think back to Jesus' saving work, **we participate in it**. As we pray at the preface of

132

Mass, "It is our duty and our salvation always and everywhere to give you thanks..." The Mass is not some empty ritual. It literally makes us present at Jesus' saving work so that the grace He won for us can fill us with His life and wipe away our sins.

10) Who gave us His own Body and Blood at the Last Supper. (P)

We finish where we began, reflecting on the pinnacle of God's plan. Sin divided us, Jesus came to make us one. The pinnacle of that plan is when we receive "Holy Communion." That phrase is exactly what happens every time we receive the Holy Eucharist. We are united to our God and to His family. When we receive Communion, we become what we eat, the Body of Christ.

The fact is, there are millions of Christians who have never received this incredible gift. And just as tragically there are millions of former Catholics who have abandoned the greatest gift in all the world; the Body and Blood of the Lord. There are millions more who, Sunday after Sunday, insult the Lord by refusing to take the time to come to His house, on His day, to gather around His altar, with His people and receive His Body and Blood.

And yet, all we need do if we have offended the Lord by staying away from this commanded food is to repent, confess and return to the table of the Lord. There we will find Jesus with open arms welcoming us back to His table!

So many things in the OT were getting the world ready for this gift. The Passover Lamb that they had to eat in order to be saved by "the blood of the lamb." The manna in the desert that was considered "bread from heaven." The Bread of the Presence that was kept on a golden table with wine and incense burning. (I highly recommend to

133

you Brant Pitre's book, *The Jewish Roots of the Eucharist* to help you understand how beautifully God was preparing the world for the Eucharist).

I could go on and on about all that God did to prepare us for this incredible gift and how blessed we are to receive the "Bread from Heaven" every time we come to Mass. But there are many other books written by people far wiser than I that are available to you. I would recommend that you regularly reflect on this most incredible gift of the Lord.

Holy Mary, Mother of God, pray for us sinners
now and at the hour of our death. Amen.

Glory be to the Father,
and to the Son, and to the Holy Spirit:
As it was in the beginning,
is now, and ever shall be, world without end. Amen

Oh my Jesus, forgive our sins and save us from the power of hell.
Lead all souls into heaven especially those
most in need of your mercy. Amen

Section 3

The

Sorrowful

Mysteries

The First Sorrowful Mystery
The Agony in the Garden

*Hail Mary, full of grace, the Lord is with you; blessed are you among women, and blessed is the fruit of your womb, **Jesus**:*

1) Who agonized over my sins. (P)

We so often can take our sins for granted, but the fact is that Jesus agonized over my sins and yours. As Catholics, we believe that if I were the only one in the world who needed saving, that Jesus would have done the very same thing to save you or me. As Catholics, we sometimes develop an attitude of, "it's only a venial sin" or we can be involved in mortal sin with the attitude of, "well, I know it's bad, but God will forgive me." Well the price of my sins and yours is the suffering and death of the Lord who loves us beyond all telling. And the only thing that the Lord wants from us in return is that we love Him. At the heart of any sin is a failure to love God who has given us everything we have and made us everything we are. When we love Him we should hate sin. That is much different than hating sinners. We are to love the sinner but hate the sin. That is also true of ourselves! It is not God's Will that we hate ourselves over our past mistakes. God wants us to rejoice in His love and mercy, while at the same time striving to overcome our sins out of love for Him.

Now, if you are anything like me, then you probably have no problem hating the sins of others, but are rather fond of your own sins. One of the biggest dangers in the spiritual life is to focus on the sins of others while being complacent of our own sins. This is one of the reasons God gave us the gift of the sacrament of reconciliation (Confession or Penance). God wants us to focus on our sins, not so that we despair over our weaknesses, but rather so that we seek to conquer sin in our own lives and we can be filled with gratitude at God's great mercy. Jesus agonized over our sins, we should never be complacent about those sins.

2) Who after singing the "great hallel" went to a garden to be tempted.

We need to understand the structure of the Last Supper to understand the dynamic here. The Last Supper was a Passover meal. The Passover was structured around four chalices of wine. Jesus gave us the Eucharist during the "third chalice" which was when the lamb was to be eaten. Matthew 26:30 states, "Then, after singing a hymn they went out to the Mount of Olives." Some Jewish scholars look at this and they laugh at the Lord. They claim Jesus messed up the Passover. The hymn is clearly the "Great hallel" (Psalm113-118). But after singing the Great hallel, the participants of the Passover should move to the fourth chalice, which is the chalice of consummation. In other words, the fourth chalice is the highpoint of the Passover. What is described in Matthew's gospel would be similar to if a priest at Mass, when the homily was finished, would say to the people, "The Mass is ended go in peace." Any faithful Catholic would respond," Father, didn't you forget something, like the most important part of the Mass?"

This is important to understand because there is a line of Jesus as He hangs on the cross that is one of the most misunderstood lines in the Bible. On the cross Jesus says, "It is finished." Many non-Catholics argue that Jesus was claiming that the work of salvation was finished, and we cannot add anything to that saving work. We will explain all of this in the chapter on the crucifixion, but for now it's essential that we make the point that the "it" that was finished was the Last Supper. Jesus had the chalice of consummation while on the cross, finishing the Last Supper.

137

It is also important to note, once again, parallels between the Fall and the work of our salvation. Adam and Eve faced temptation in a garden and chose to disobey God. Jesus will face temptation in the garden on the Mount of Olives but will choose to be obedient unto death.

3) Who said to the Apostles, "Watch and pray that you may not be put to the test."

The only thing the Apostles watched was the inside of their eyelids. They did not devote themselves to prayer while Jesus was agonizing over the sins of the world. The result was that they were put to the test and, just about everyone would agree, that it was a test they failed miserably. Jesus implies that with prayer things could have been different. I know in my own life a failure to be faithful in prayer has often led to poor choices. We need to strive to be faithful in prayer.

4) Who prayed, "Father if you are willing, take this cup away from me...."

We have already seen how, after drinking the third cup of the Passover meal the Lord and His Apostles sang the Great hallel and without having the fourth cup, went out to the garden. Here Jesus prays for a cup to be taken away. This again is important for us to understand what happened on the cross and why Jesus will say, "It is finished." Jesus is to have the fourth cup on the cross finishing the Last Supper.

5) Who prayed, "... not my will, but yours be done."

Here, Jesus is the perfect model of prayer. Too often we pray in the hopes of changing God's mind. We pray with the hope that God will do things our way. And often, when He does not do things our way, we get angry at Him. How many people do you personally know who have abandoned faith because God did not answer their prayers the

138

way they wanted them answered? There are many. In fact, as Dinesh D'Souza points out, many of the "new atheists" are not really atheists at all; they are wounded theists. It's not that they really do not believe in God; their atheism is a striking out at the God who has disappointed them. But Jesus shows us the attitude we should have when we pray. An attitude of humility that basically says, "God, whatever happens, I know you want what is best and I will entrust myself and my loved ones to your providence." We can certainly ask, as Jesus did, for things to go in ways that are more consistent with our hopes and dreams, but the bottom line is that God's Wisdom is far beyond ours. God's plans are greater than our plans, for as we read in Isaiah 55:8-9:

> *For my thoughts are not your thoughts, nor are your ways My ways. For as the heavens are higher than the earth so are My ways higher than your ways, My thoughts higher than your thoughts.*

It takes trust in the Lord and a humble attitude to place our lives in His hands, but that is what faith calls us to do. The prayer of Jesus should remind all of us that the Wisdom of God is far greater than our hopes and desires. There are words of wisdom that say, "If you want to make God laugh, tell Him your plans." The corollary to that is, "Life is what happens to you as you are making other plans."

The fact is that each of our lives is an adventure, a gift from God. We should have the attitude of the character Reepicheep, the valiant mouse in CS Lewis' book *The Voyage of the Dawn Treader* who said as they were to embark on a perilous journey, "Let us go and embrace the adventure that Aslan sends us" (Aslan is the Christ figure in the book). Jesus embraced the Father's plan and brought salvation to the world. When we embrace God's plans for our lives, we too can do great

139

things for the Lord, but we need the attitude of, "not my will, but yours be done."

6) Who sweat blood over my sins.

Once again, we see Jesus agonizing over my sins and yours. As we contemplate His agony, we should all be moved to strive to overcome our sins which caused His suffering. Scientists tell us that sweating blood is possible when the person is under great stress. The clinical term is hematohidrosis, and it is caused by blood vessels constricting to the point of rupture and the blood getting into the sweat glands. There is no doubt that Jesus was in great agony as He contemplated what was necessary for the redemption of the world.

This also is related to the punishment that God gave our first parents at the Fall. In Genesis 3:19 God says to Adam, *By the sweat of your face shall you get bread to eat until you return to the ground from which you were taken; for you are dirt and to dirt you shall return.* In saving us, Jesus sweats blood, taking our punishment upon Himself.

7) Who said to the Apostles, "Could you not watch one hour?"

This line from Mark 14:37 is one that I fear many modern Catholics will hear Jesus say on the Day of Judgment. God gives us 168 hours every week and He only demands that we spend one of those hours in His house, on His day, with His people, around His altar, to receive His Body and Blood; and yet many today cannot be bothered. As we spoke before in the chapter on the Last Supper, the Eucharist is the source and summit of our faith, it is not some minor aspect of faith.

I have heard many ask, "You think God won't let me into heaven just because I missed Mass?" I usually answer, "No, God won't let you in

140

heaven because you don't love Him." The fact is the whole reason we have life is to know, love and serve God. Jesus tells us that the first command of faith is that we love God with all our heart, all our soul, all our mind, and all our strength. The Bible tells us in Galatians 5:6 that we are saved by faith working in love. Well if we have the Catholic faith we believe that Jesus is truly present body, blood, soul and divinity in the Holy Eucharist. If we love Him, we will make every reasonable effort to be there to receive Him.

The question, "Will I go to hell for missing Mass" is not the question that love asks. The motivation behind that question is an attitude that basically says, "What's the least I have to do to get to heaven? I don't want to get too involved in faith, *so what's the least I have to do?*" Many people have asked that of themselves and concluded, "God won't keep me out of heaven for missing Mass." Millions miss Mass regularly. *But the questions love asks is*, "**God, what do you want me to do? How can I please you?**" When we ask those questions, we will get a completely different answer than when we ask, "What's the least I have to do?" Does God want us to come together with His family? Of course, He does! Does God want us to receive the very body, blood, soul, and divinity of His Son regularly? Of course, He does! Does God want us to obey Jesus' command of "Do this in memory of me?" Of course, He does!

When we ask the right questions, we will get the right answer when it comes to salvation. Please ask the right questions. I know as a priest one of the most difficult tasks I have is to celebrate the funeral of someone who does not regularly attend Mass. While I always want to give hope, since of course I cannot judge the state of an individual's soul, it is a difficult balancing act. While I want to give hope, I do not want to give the false impression that the person's failure to obey the command of the Lord is no big deal. In staying away from Mass, a

141

person puts themselves in great danger. We do not want to hear Jesus say to us, "could you not watch for one hour?"

8) Who said to the Apostles, "...the spirit is willing, but the flesh is weak."

The Lord is not making excuses for the Apostles here, He is chastising them. Yes, the flesh is weak, but with God's grace we can grow strong. They had an opportunity to open their hearts to God's grace, but they did not. The good news, of course, is that they eventually did. All the remaining Apostles died martyrs except St. John, who died in exile. They all with God's grace became wonderful men of faith.

Whatever your weaknesses and struggles, know that with God's grace you too can become a saint. Our Christian faith is so filled with hope! If we have neglected the table of the Lord all we need do is repent, confess and we will find Jesus with open arms welcoming us to His holy table on earth as well as in heaven!

9) Who was betrayed by the kiss of a friend.

My first thought on this is Kevin C who lived in my neighborhood when I was a boy. Kevin was a boy from Scotland who moved onto my street when I was a child. I met him and liked him. But a lot of the other kids on the street rejected him, perhaps because of his accent. Wanting to be accepted I joined the gang and rejected Kevin as well. I betrayed a friend and I think of him (and pray for him) every time I come to this reflection. In that circumstance, I was Judas.

Are there people who have betrayed me? Absolutely, I try not to dwell on that. Those times of betrayal give me a small insight into what

142

Jesus went through for me. In those cases, I try to unite my pain at betrayal to the suffering of Jesus.

While Kevin is the only one that I ever remember betraying, the truth is I have also let people down. Usually this is not the result of bad will on my part, but I have let people down nonetheless. Whether it be from laziness, or inattention, or fear, or just plain forgetfulness, I have hurt people and for that I am truly sorry. I, of course, have also disappointed God through my sins. But as I ponder these things it makes me aware of the incredible mercy of our Lord. Peter disappointed Jesus, but He still made him the head of His Church. The other Apostles abandoned Him in His time of need, but Jesus still gave them the privilege of carrying on His saving work. Saul the Pharisee disappointed God, but He still called him to become Paul the Apostle. Judas betrayed Jesus and then confounded the problem by believing that his sin was greater than Jesus' love. We never want to be like Judas. We certainly never want to betray a friend, nor do we want to falsely believe that our sins are greater than the love of the Lord. Judas could have been forgiven if he had simply repented. That is all it takes for any of us.

As you pray this 9th bead of the first sorrowful mystery, I would caution you against dwelling on those you feel have betrayed you. If you must think of them, ask God's mercy for them. It certainly would be counter- productive to this beautiful prayer if we allowed anger, bitterness or resentment to enter our hearts because of this reflection.

10) Who agonized over the sins of the world. (P)

We again end as we started. At the beginning, we focused on how Jesus agonized over our personal sins. Now we reflect on how we are all in this together. We are all sinners in need of God's mercy. Jesus died for all sinners. While some will not repent of their sins and come to the mercy of God, Jesus always has the door open to us. As we rejoice in His incredible mercy, we want to remember that Jesus invites those who have hurt us into His mercy as well. We do not want to be like the Pharisees who thought they could judge who was worthy of God's love and who was not. They were shocked at those Jesus chose to love. Since Jesus did not limit His love, we should not limit ours either.

Holy Mary, Mother of God, pray for us sinners
now and at the hour of our death. Amen.

Glory be to the Father,
and to the Son, and to the Holy Spirit:
As it was in the beginning,
is now, and ever shall be, world without end. Amen

Oh my Jesus, forgive our sins and save us from the power of hell.
Lead all souls into heaven especially those
most in need of your mercy. Amen

The Second Sorrowful Mystery
The Scourging at the Pillar

*Hail Mary, full of grace, the Lord is with you; blessed are you among women, and blessed is the fruit of your womb, **Jesus**:*

1) Who suffered an agonizing scourging for my sins. (P)

If you saw Mel Gibson's movie *The Passion of the Christ*, you most likely remember the scourging at the pillar. It was one of the most powerful scenes in the film. The scourging was incredibly brutal. What Jesus endured for my salvation and yours is beyond words. But Jesus endured incredible brutality out of love for you and me. Bill O'Reilly in his book *Killing Jesus* points out how Roman scourgings often left people near death with their inner organs exposed. As I mentioned earlier, we often take our sins for granted. The scourging at the pillar is a strong reminder of the price of our forgiveness. When we see what Jesus endured for sin, we should hate sin (not sinners, but sin).

2) Who was found guilty of blasphemy by the Sanhedrin.

There are so many aspects of the Passion of Jesus, we need to go beyond the words of the rosary mysteries and examine all that Jesus endured. He was brought before the legal authority of the Jewish people for judgment and they found Him guilty. Nowhere in this action do we see Jesus say that they have forfeited their authority because of what they have decided. Jesus allowed the lawful authority of His people to judge Him, even though they judged Him falsely. We have seen previously how Jesus, though God, submitted to lawful human authority over Him. This is one more example of Jesus accepting the Divine authority of the Sanhedrin even though they promulgated a gross injustice upon Him. The example of Jesus certainly makes clear that God wants each of us to submit to the lawful authority over us. It is important to contemplate this since we live in a society that basically says, "No one can judge me." Jesus allowed the Sanhedrin to judge Him. He allowed their lawful judgment to be carried out even though it was a great travesty of justice.

3) Who was brought before Pilate, then Herod and back to Pilate for judgment.

Jesus does not plead for mercy. He does not threaten them with damnation. He once again allows the authority of government officials to determine His fate. It was a horrific fate, but the Lord does not protest.

Jesus, for the most part, remains silent before His judges. The Bible tells us that God has given authority to governments. Let's take a look at Rom 13:1-7:

> *Let every person be subordinate to the higher authorities, for there is no authority except from God, and those that exist have*

been established by God. Therefore, whoever resists authority opposes what God has appointed, and those who oppose it will bring judgment upon themselves. For rulers are not a cause of fear to good conduct, but to evil. Do you wish to have no fear of authority? Then do what is good and you will receive approval from it, for it is a servant of God for your good. But if you do evil, be afraid, for it does not bear the sword without purpose; it is the servant of God to inflict wrath on the evildoer. Therefore, it is necessary to be subject not only because of the wrath but also because of conscience. This is why you also pay taxes, for the authorities are ministers of God, devoting themselves to this very thing. Pay to all their dues, taxes to whom taxes are due, toll to whom toll is due, respect to whom respect is due, honor to whom honor is due.

Even though Rome was a brutal and dictatorial ruler, they had authority that comes from God. Jesus submits to that authority. Pilate and Herod were not good men, but Jesus submits. If we are to follow Jesus' example we also must submit to lawful authority, even though we will at times find that authority unjust.

4) Who said to Pilate, "For this I was born. For this I came into the world, to testify to the truth. Everyone who belongs to the truth hears my voice."

Do you belong to the truth? Do you hear the voice of Jesus? Many Christians today do not. The Bible makes it very clear that there is a source we can turn to in order to hear the voice of Jesus, but most Christians do not want to hear that voice. The Bible is clear that we can know the truth, but most Christians today have the attitude of "pick a belief, any belief." Despite the promises of Jesus that we could know the truth, most followers of the Lord would rather follow their own opinions or the spirit of the age, than listen to the one source that God Himself guarantees is the pillar and bulwark of all truth (see 1 Tim 3:15). We see once again how sinful pride stands in the way of people embracing the fullness of truth that Jesus died on the cross to share with us. In the last section of the book we will deal more thoroughly with the issue of where we can hear the voice of the Lord and find the truth through His Holy Catholic Church.

5) Who received 39 lashes with the whip.

This is a best guess since the scriptures do not tell us how many lashes Jesus received. The traditional number of lashes was 39. We see this in the life of St. Paul when he tells us in 2 Cor 11:24 that five times he received 39 lashes. But again, we do not know this for sure.

6) Who was scourged with a whip that had three cords.

7) Who was scourged with a whip that had bone and metal imbedded that was designed to rip the flesh.

The whip most likely used on Jesus was called a "flagellum" or "flagrum." The historian Eusebius described a scourging with a flagellum in the following way, "For they say that the bystanders were struck with amazement when they saw them lacerated with scourges even to the innermost veins and arteries, so that the hidden inward parts of the body, both their bowels and their members, were exposed to view" (Ecclesiastical History, Book 4, chap. 15). It was so brutal that Roman citizens could not receive this punishment. It was meant to humiliate and debase the person scourged.

The Shroud of Turin gives indications that Jesus was scourged with this kind of brutal weapon. The image on the Shroud points to a man

148

who had more than 100 deep lacerations. Jesus suffered a humiliating experience at the hands of the Romans. It is once again a reminder to us of how serious sin is.

8) Whose scourging fulfilled scripture.

The prophet Isaiah spoke of the suffering servant who would take away the sins of the world, including the scourging of the Lord. In Isaiah 53:1-12 we read:

> *Who would believe what we have heard? To whom has the arm of the LORD been revealed? He grew up like a sapling before him like a shoot from the parched earth; He had no majestic bearing to catch our eye, no beauty to draw us to him. He was spurned and avoided by men, a man of suffering, knowing pain, like one from whom you turn your face, spurned, and we held him in no esteem. Yet it was our pain that he bore, our sufferings he endured. We thought of him as stricken, struck down by God and afflicted, but he was pierced for our sins, crushed for our iniquity. He bore the punishment that makes us whole, **by his wounds we were healed.** We had all gone astray like sheep, all following our own way; But the LORD laid upon him the guilt of us all. Though harshly treated, he submitted and did not open his mouth; Like a lamb led to slaughter or a sheep silent before shearers, he did not open his mouth. Seized and condemned, he was taken away. Who would have thought any more of his destiny? For he was cut off from the land of the living, struck for the sins of his people. He was given a grave among the wicked, a burial place with evildoers, though he had done no wrong, nor was deceit found in his mouth. But it was the LORD's will to crush him with pain. By making his life as a reparation offering he shall see his offspring, shall lengthen his days, and the LORD's will shall be accomplished through him.*

149

Because of his anguish he shall see the light; because of his knowledge he shall be content;

My servant, the just one, shall justify the many, their iniquity he shall bear. Therefore, I will give him his portion among the many, and he shall divide the spoils with the mighty, because he surrendered himself to death, was counted among the transgressors, Bore the sins of many, and interceded for the transgressor"

In verse 5 this translation says, ".... by his wounds we are healed." Most translations say, "by his stripes we are healed." Stripes is a reference to the scourging that the Lord would undergo. So the King of kings undergoes this brutal torture for your sins and mine.

9) Whose scourging shows man's inhumanity to man.

The Roman Empire was brutal. Roughly 1/3 of all the people in the Empire were slaves living in unimaginable conditions with almost no hope. People fled to Roman arenas to see gladiators kill one another, or later on to see Christians fed to the lions. People would give a thumbs up or thumbs down indicating whether they thought the losing gladiator should be killed—all for sport.

Mighty Rome also dealt with troublesome people in extraordinarily brutal fashion. Crucifixions were commonplace. At times the Romans would crucify entire towns and have the crosses along miles of highways in order to be a warning to others to not challenge the authority of the Empire.

So how did we go from that to a society that sees, as the Declaration of Independence states, that it is self-evident that the Creator endowed people with certain inalienable rights? How did we go from a culture of slavery to one where slavery is outlawed? The answer is Jesus! **Jesus changes everything!** The message of the gospel transformed western civilization and since western civilization is the dominant one in the world, it has transformed the world. When Jesus taught us to love our neighbor as ourselves; when He taught, "Whatever you do to the least of my brothers or sisters you do to me." When He taught us to forgive others and to not seek revenge; when He taught one man, one woman for life; Jesus changed everything. In Christian lands we see kings and queens coming off their thrones going into the streets to minister to the poor and sick. No such thing ever happened in ancient Rome, or Babylon, or any other ancient empire. Jesus transformed our world for the better!

But now as our civilization pulls away from Jesus we see brutality increasing. Every day in the United States more than 3,000 unborn babies are killed and many do not even give it a second thought. We have presidents and senators and Supreme Court justices speak of that slaughter as "a right." Throughout the world we have seen genocide and horrendous wars. Adolph Hitler hated Christianity and he unleashed policies and a war that killed tens of millions of people. Stalin pushing his atheistic agenda killed roughly 30 million of his own citizens and imposed totalitarian rule over the entire Soviet Empire. Mao's "cultural revolution" in China killed between 50-70 million people. In comparison with them, Pol Pot's Khmer Rouge in Cambodia were just a bunch of pikers. After all they "only" killed three million people. Folks, without Jesus, respect for human life diminishes greatly. After all, what is it that gives human beings dignity? It is the fact that we are made in the image and likeness of God. It is the fact that Jesus taught that what we do to others we do to Him and we will come before Him for judgment someday. But for

151

those who do not believe in God, then humans are no different than cows or pigs and chickens--- and we kill them all the time!

The Christians of our country need to wake up. We have people insisting that the teaching of Jesus should have no part in our laws or our culture. Many of the same people keep pushing for bigger and bigger government. We have seen throughout the world how compassionate governments are without Jesus. They are brutal! In our country we see those who would push Jesus out of the public square lie, deceive, and use the politics of personal destruction. The secular left have no moral compass and will seek to crush anyone who is opposed to them. As we continue to raise children who do not know Jesus, as we continue to keep Christian values out of our laws, we are heading toward brutality.

Jesus suffered an agonizing scourging at the hands of a godless all-powerful government. Human nature has not changed. Many today feel, "that couldn't happen here," but it already is. As I mentioned the slaughter of the unborn, government mandates that Christian business owners cover things in their medical plans that violate their conscience, the government is now limiting the amount of medical care the elderly can receive—it's already happening. Only with God's Wisdom and God's grace can that fallen human nature be held in check. 80% of Americans claim to be Christian. We need to stand up for a Christian civilization or we will instead live under brutal totalitarianism.

10) Who suffered an agonizing scourging for the redemption of the world. (P)

We end where we began, only at the beginning we focused on how Jesus suffered this brutality for our personal sins. Now we focus on how His saving work brought redemption to the whole world. Sin has a very heavy price; we should hate our sins and strive to overcome them.

*Holy Mary, Mother of God, pray for us sinners
now and at the hour of our death. Amen.*

*Glory be to the Father,
and to the Son, and to the Holy Spirit:
As it was in the beginning,
is now, and ever shall be, world without end. Amen*

*Oh my Jesus, forgive our sins and save us from the power of hell.
Lead all souls into heaven especially those
most in need of your mercy. Amen*

The Third Sorrowful Mystery
The Crowning with Thorns

*Hail Mary, full of grace, the Lord is with you; blessed are you among women, and blessed is the fruit of your womb, **Jesus:***

1) God's eternal truth who was mocked. (P)

Jesus is the way the truth and the light. Jesus is the all-powerful second person of the Blessed Trinity. Jesus is not only the "King of the Jews" but is the "King of kings." And yet the truth was mocked, laughed at, ridiculed. Think of the Roman guards who mocked Him believing Him to be an insignificant nobody; think of the crowd who yelled out for Barabbas to be released rather than Jesus; think of Pilate and Herod who had the power to save Him, but refused; and yet they would each one day come before Him for judgment. We see throughout history, especially recent history how the truth continues to be mocked and derided. At the end of this chapter we will examine more clearly how the truth proclaimed by God's Holy Church is mocked today.

2) Who had a crown of thorns placed on His sacred head, fulfilling scripture.

So much of what Jesus did for our salvation goes back to the Fall. Jesus had to undo the sin of our first parents. He had to take the punishment given to them and their descendants upon Himself. So we see in Genesis 3:17b-18 that God said to Adam, *Cursed be the ground because of you! In toil shall you eat its yield all the days of your life. Thorns and thistles shall it bring forth to you as you eat of the plants of the field.* Here we see Jesus take the punishment of thorns upon Himself.

3) Who had a robe of royal purple placed over His shoulders.

4) Before whom the guards fell on their knees, mockingly saying, "Hail, King of the Jews."

The laughter and mockery continues. The Roman soldiers were having a good old time at the expense of this man they thought was an insignificant Jewish preacher. They served mighty Rome and no one who claimed to be a king outside the confines of the Roman power structure could be tolerated. Rome was all powerful and anyone who would threaten the Empire in even the slightest way would be crushed. Their mockery served two purposes; it not only relieved the burden of their daily grind, but it also served to add to the humiliation, so that no one who saw this, would ever think of challenging the Roman authorities.

5) Who is the King of the Jews.

6) Who is the King of Kings.

The Roman soldiers and the Jewish crowd had no idea whom they were laughing at and mocking. They thought Him to be a foolish preacher who got a little too big for His britches. They thought that this itinerant preacher would soon be forgotten. And yet no person has had greater impact on world history than the man they ridiculed. No emperor, no king, no president nor prime minister has even come close to the transformation that Jesus brought to the world. Jesus and His Holy Church have brought a transformation of which the ancient Rome could never have dreamt.

Earlier we spoke of those who, for the sake of the Kingdom of God, have left everything worldly and taken vows of poverty, chastity and obedience to serve Jesus and build up His Kingdom. These men and women, inspired by the Lord, brought education to the masses, brought about the beginning of hospitals and began the University systems of the world. Without Jesus and His faithful followers, the world would be a much different place than it is today. Jesus who was cruelly mocked is the eternal truth of God.

7) Who heard Pilate say to the crowd, 'Behold the man."

Pilate believed Jesus to be an innocent man. His wife had warned him about her dream that he should do no harm to this preacher. But Pilate had to be concerned about his career. It was the time of Passover and Jerusalem was filled with people. The Jewish leaders were insisting that this preacher be killed. Pilate had already been reprimanded by Rome because of the past insurrections of the Jews; one more time and he might lose everything. So Pilate hopes against hope that a brutal beating of Jesus will be enough to satisfy the Jewish leaders and the crowd. He presents Jesus to them so that they can see that this man is powerless and will not be a threat to anyone. No one suffering such a brutal beating, such heartless humiliation, would ever dare to step out of line again.

Pilate has the power of mighty Rome behind him and yet is filled with fear that these unruly subjects might cost him everything. To him, Jesus was not so much a man, but a problem. And if a troublesome preacher had to suffer a brutal death to protect his place in Roman society, oh well.

8) Who heard the crowd yell, "Crucify Him. Crucify Him."

The Jewish leaders hated Jesus. He had challenged them, tripped them up as they sought to lay traps for Him, and embarrassed them. They certainly were not going to give up now when what they had plotted, hoped for, desired was about to occur. No, they were not going to let Jesus or Pilate off the hook. They knew that Jerusalem was overflowing with the crowds for Passover. They knew that Pilate was a cowardly man who needed to keep the peace. They had both Pilate and Jesus right where they wanted them and nothing was going to persuade them to back down now. Let's take a look at this as it appears in John 19:1-16

> *Then Pilate took Jesus and had him scourged. And the soldiers wove a crown out of thorns and placed it on his head, and clothed him in a purple cloak, and they came to him and said, "Hail, King of the Jews!" And they struck him repeatedly. Once more Pilate went out and said to them, "Look, I am bringing him out to you, so that you may know that I find no guilt in him." So Jesus came out, wearing the crown of thorns and the purple cloak. And he said to them, "Behold, the man!" When the chief priests and the guards saw him they cried out, "Crucify him, crucify him!" Pilate said to them, "Take him yourselves and crucify him. I find no guilt in him." **The Jews answered, "We have a law, and according to that law he ought to die, because he made himself the Son of God."** Now when Pilate heard this statement, he became even more afraid, and went back into the praetorium and said to Jesus, "Where are you from?" Jesus did not answer him. So Pilate said to him, "Do you not speak to me? Do you not know that I have power to release you and I have power to crucify you?" Jesus answered [him], "You would have no power over me if it had not been given to you from above. For this reason the one who handed me over to you has the greater sin." Consequently, Pilate tried to release him; but the Jews cried out, "If you release him, you are not a friend of Caesar.*

Everyone who makes himself a king opposes Caesar." When Pilate heard these words he brought Jesus out and seated him on the judge's bench in the place called Stone Pavement, in Hebrew, Gabbatha. It was preparation day for Passover, and it was about noon. And he said to the Jews, "Behold, your king!" They cried out, "Take him away, take him away! Crucify him!" Pilate said to them, "Shall I crucify your king?" The chief priests answered, "We have no king but Caesar." Then he handed him over to them to be crucified.

Other than St. John, we do not know if any of the Apostles were there. Jesus' mother was there. Mary Magdalene was there. What did they feel as the one they loved, believed in, had hoped in, was rejected by His own people? When they heard the words, "crucify Him, crucify Him" their hearts must have sunk.

I know there are times my spirits have sunk with disappointment when others have been indifferent or even hostile to innocent life. These experiences usually happen to me the day after an election when I read that the majority of Catholics voted for the person who promised to work hard so that the slaughter of the unborn could continue in our country. It's as if millions of people with their votes have yelled, "Crucify them, crucify them." The brutality of the Roman Empire is being resurrected with the votes of many who claim to be followers of the Lord.

But again, even if we, in the past, stood with those who allow the slaughter of the unborn, we need only repent, confess and turn to the Lord to receive His incredible mercy in our lives. It is my hope and prayer that all Christians and all men and women of good will one day

158

stand for the dignity of all life from the moment of conception to the time of natural death.

9) Who heard the high priest say, "We have no king but Caesar."

In the above passage from St. John we were told how the chief priests said, "We have no king but Caesar." Jesus was condemned for "blasphemy," but anyone familiar with the books of the OT would recognize the most vile of blasphemies being uttered by the high priests. The OT makes it clear that the true "king of the Jews" was God Himself. In fact for the first several centuries after the Israelites had entered the Promised Land they did not have a king. Various "judges" ruled over them for a time, but there was no king. The people saw God as their king.

But the people of Israel wanted to be "like the nations" who all had human kings ruling over them. When God allowed them to have an earthly king, the king was seen as a servant of the Lord. King Saul, their first king failed in his service to the Lord. God then had David anointed to be their king and promised that a descendant of David would always rule over the Israelites. But as time went on, the Northern ten tribes rebelled against David's grandson and established a separate nation. Centuries later the Babylonians conquered Judah and killed the sons of the reigning monarch. It appeared that the king in the line of David was lost forever, but God had preserved David's line.

In the time of Jesus, the people were expecting the Messiah who would be a king in the line of David. When the high priests say, "We have no king but Caesar" they are denying God Himself and making a mockery of the promise of God that a king in the line of David would soon appear.

10) God's eternal truth who was mocked. (P)

God's eternal truth is mocked. But the more things change, the more they stay the same. Many today mock the teaching of the Catholic Church on the sacredness of sexuality; her ban against contraception and her teaching that the deepest form of human sharing is to take place only between a man and woman, united by God in the holy sacrament of marriage.

The Catholic Church teaches that it is a serious sin to treat our fertility (which is an incredible gift of God) as if it is a disease. She teaches that there are two inseparable aspects of sexual sharing, the unitive power and the pro-creative power. While everyone recognizes those two powers, many in our time choose to suppress the pro-creative power. Back in the 1960s when the birth control pill first became available to the public, many were saying, "Thank God we have finally separated love making from baby making." The problem with that attitude was that God had put them together! And as time goes by it is more and more clear that in destroying the pro-creative power of sexuality, we destroy its unitive power as well.

Pope Paul VI had warned of several dangers if contraception became acceptable as a way of solving personal problems. 1) He warned that a wide path for immorality would be opened; 2) he warned that men would come to see women no longer as a trusted partner, but as objects to use for their own selfish ends; and finally 3) he said that if couples see contraception as a way of solving their personal problems, then nations would begin to force contraception on their people to solve their national problems. Everything Pope Paul warned us of has occurred. There certainly has been a downward spiral of morality, especially in the area of sexuality. More and more men have become exploiters of women rather than protectors of women. We see that exploitation in pornography, strip clubs and human trafficking for the sex trade.

Back in the 1960s there were others who were trying to get the Church to change her teachings. They painted the picture of a "contraceptive paradise." They argued that contraception would strengthen marriages because men and women could share their love more freely without the fear of unwanted pregnancy. They said that contraception would lead to fewer out –of- wedlock births (the rate of out of wedlock births in the early 60s was 5%--it is 42% now) as people would have "protected sex," and people would be so much happier as a result of all this worry -free love making.

Who was right? Pope Paul VI or those who painted the picture of a contraceptive paradise? The fact is, in treating a gift of God like a disease, in treating sexuality, which God tells us is sacred, as if it is some cheap form of entertainment, in ignoring the Wisdom of God in the area of sexuality we have opened a Pandora's box of heartache and pain, and yet people still mock the Church for her teaching.

With the collapse of sexual morality more and more woman and their children live in poverty. Many young girls in high school, if they are to be popular, if they are to be taken seriously, if they are to have a boyfriend; they must allow guys to use them. We have whole neighborhoods where the out- of- wedlock birth rates are 72%; those communities are filled with poverty, crime, drugs, hopelessness and despair. A large preponderance of our prison population was raised without fathers, and yet there are many who mock the Catholic Church and say that the "Church must get with the times."

The fact is, if we are to turn our broken culture around, the times need to get with the Church. In ignoring the wisdom of God our culture has unleashed a flood of filth, hopelessness and despair upon our world. As the truth is mocked, more and more people, especially young people, suffer as a result.

Jesus who is God's eternal truth was mocked on the day of His Passion; the truth continues to be mocked today as the infallible teaching of His Church is ignored.

Holy Mary, Mother of God, pray for us sinners
now and at the hour of our death. Amen.

Glory be to the Father,
and to the Son, and to the Holy Spirit:
As it was in the beginning,
is now, and ever shall be, world without end. Amen

Oh my Jesus, forgive our sins and save us from the power of hell.
Lead all souls into heaven especially those
most in need of your mercy. Amen

The Fourth Sorrowful Mystery
Jesus Carries His Cross

*Hail Mary, full of grace, the Lord is with you; blessed are you among women, and blessed is the fruit of your womb, **Jesus**:*

1) Who carried the cross for my salvation. (P)

Jesus loves me and did the unthinkable to save me. Jesus loves you, too. It boggles the mind that the all-powerful God, the One who is the Word spoken by the Father through whom all of creation came into existence, could love creatures as weak and seemingly insignificant as us, but He does. He did this so that you and I could be forgiven. This is the cost of our sin, and yet we often sin (at least I do) with little thought of the cost of redemption. Sin is no small matter!

2) Who was to be nailed to a tree because our first parents sinned at a tree. (P)

This reflection gives us the opportunity to contemplate the big picture of God's saving work. First of all, it calls us to reflect upon the parallels between the Fall and Salvation. It also allows us to reflect on much in the OT that was pointing us to the cross.

In the Book of Genesis, we are told of creation and the Fall. We saw in the Joyful Mysteries the nature of the test that God gave to our first parents. We saw that, rather than being tricked by a little snake, they were really intimidated by the dragon. We saw that they sinned at a tree. Adam had the option of eating from the tree of life and then stand between the dragon and his bride protecting her, but he failed to do so. Sin came into the world at the "tree of the knowledge of good and evil." In saving us Jesus is nailed to the "tree of life." Adam refused to lay down his life for his bride, but Jesus does lay down His life for His bride, the Church.

But there are other OT stories that point us to Jesus being lifted up on the cross which is good for us to reflect on here. In Numbers 21 we are told the story of the Israelites complaining against God and the Lord sends seraph serpents to bite the people and many died. When Moses intercedes for them, God tells him to mount a serpent on a pole and whoever looks at the serpent on the pole will be healed. Jesus tells us that this was pointing to Him in John 3:14 when He says, *"And just as Moses lifted up the serpent in the desert, so must the Son of Man be lifted up, so that everyone who believes in him may have eternal life."*

Notice Jesus says the serpent was "lifted up." In Numbers the people had to look at the serpent in order to be healed. Jesus will be lifted up and everyone who looks on Him with faith will be saved.

Have you ever looked at the Lord lifted up? As Catholics every time we come to Mass we see Jesus lifted up over the altar. When we look on Him with faith we will be healed.

Another event in the life of Israel that was pointing us to the cross occurs in Exodus 15:25 when we are told, *"As the people grumbled against Moses, saying, "What are we to drink?" he cried out to the LORD, who pointed out to him a piece of wood. When he threw it into the water, the water became fresh."*

This points us to the cross and the sacrament of baptism. In Exodus the water by itself could not save the people because it was too bitter. But with the wood it is able to save them. Water by itself has no power to

164

save us, but by the wood of the cross, the waters of baptism can now convey to us God's saving grace.

3) Who was given the cross because Pilate washed his hands of His (Jesus') fate.

Pilate believed Jesus to be an innocent man and did not want Him to be crucified. But you might say that Pilate was "pro-choice" when it came to the crucifixion of the Lord. He was "personally opposed" but he could not "force his morality" on the people who were yelling "crucify Him, crucify Him."

Sadly, today there are many Christians who identify themselves as "pro-choice." When it comes to the destruction of innocent babies before birth they, like Pilate, are "personally opposed," but they cannot "force their morality" on others. They have the same moral courage as Pontius Pilate.

I personally believe that Pontius Pilate was one of the most gutless, despicable men in history. He washed his hands, but that does not make him innocent of the blood of the Lord. Those who take the "Pontius Pilate approach to abortion" also have innocent blood on their hands. Jesus taught us that whatever we do to the least of our brothers or sisters, we do to Him. Those who identify themselves as "pro-choice" are allowing the destruction of Jesus in every abortion that their indifference allows to occur.

In all honesty my disgust for Pontius Pilate probably comes from my fear that I am a lot like him. What would I have done if my career and possibly my life was hanging in the balance? I would hope that I would stand up for innocent life, but I am not sure. I have often lacked the courage to do the right thing. The fact is, in this situation, Pontius

Pilate was a coward who allowed innocent blood to be spilled. No Christian should ever seek to imitate him! The good news, of course, is that even if we have taken the "Pontius Pilate approach to abortion" in the past, we can repent, confess and be received into the waiting arms of the Lord who reaches out to each of us with such incredible mercy!

4) Who fell again and again and again under the weight of my sins.

Jesus fell under the weight of our sins. We often fall under the weight of our personal sins. But Jesus here is our model on how to act when we fall into sin: we are to get back up and move forward. Jesus did not give up when He fell; He got up and kept going, we are to do the same.

5) Who met His Blessed Mother along the way.

The scriptures are clear that Mary very much shared in the suffering of her Son. Going back to the 4th Joyful Mystery when Simeon foretold that Mary's soul would be pierced with the sword of sorrow, Mary was to cooperate in Jesus' redemption of the world. She was there to support Him as He was "obedient unto death." This contrasts greatly with the original woman who encouraged the original Adam to disobey God. Here Mary is present to support Jesus as He willingly sacrifices His earthly life in order to overcome the sin of Adam. As Eve encouraged Adam to sin, Mary now encourages the new Adam as He conquers sin.

6) Who was helped to carry His cross by Simon.

7) Whose bloody faced was wiped by Veronica.

166

Here we have two examples, one biblical and one that comes to us from tradition, of people helping Jesus to carry the cross. But since Jesus is God, why would He need any help?

This gives us great insight into God's plan of salvation. The fact is, we are not meant to be passive recipients of the gift of salvation, but active participants. God in His love has made us co-workers with Jesus. That is why St. Paul in Colossians 1:24-25 says, *"Now I rejoice in my sufferings for your sake, and in my flesh, I am filling up what is lacking in the afflictions of Christ on behalf of his body, which is the church, of which I am a minister in accordance with God's stewardship given to me to bring to completion for you the word of God...*

Here the scriptures are telling us that God has elevated us to be co-workers with Jesus. Our lives matter when it comes to the work of salvation. Our suffering matters! Our stewardship matters. Why? Because you and I are members of the body of Christ. And while we are saved by the suffering of Christ, St. Paul makes it clear that Jesus continues to suffer through His body; through you and through me. And His suffering through His body continues to make present the grace of salvation.

This insight into the work of salvation is one that many outside the Catholic Church miss. But this insight is essential to grasp if we are to understand the work of salvation and to take our place in "helping Jesus" as Simon and Veronica did.

8) **Who said to the women of Jerusalem, "Don't weep for me, but for yourselves and your children."**

167

Jesus loved the people of Jerusalem even though many did not love Him. Jesus had foretold the destruction of Jerusalem. In Luke 19:41-44 we read,

> *As he drew near, he saw the city and wept over it, saying, "If this day you only knew what makes for peace—but now it is hidden from your eyes. For the days are coming upon you when your enemies will raise a palisade against you; they will encircle you and hem you in on all sides. They will smash you to the ground and your children within you, and they will not leave one stone upon another within you because you did not recognize the time of your visitation.*

While there would be consequences for the city of Jerusalem, Jesus mourned for the people who would suffer. Even the followers of Jesus would have their lives very much disrupted. We know from history that no Christians were present in Jerusalem when the city was destroyed by the Roman Empire in 70AD, because the Christians all fled. Jesus had warned them what was coming. But even the lives of the Christians were disrupted. Here we see the compassion of Jesus who, even in the midst of His Passion, is concerned with the suffering of others.

9) Who was stripped of His clothing.

In "Everyone's Way of the Cross" the tenth station reads, "Behold the poorest king who ever lived." It goes on to speak of how He is stripped before His people and even the cross is not His own. But it concludes, "...yet who has ever been so rich? Possessing His Father's love, He has everything." This was all part of the humiliation of crucifixion.

168

This is just one more reminder of all that Jesus did out of love for you and me

10) Who carried His cross for the salvation of the world. (P)

We again end as we began. Jesus carried His cross for you and for me. The depth of His love is beyond words, but it is about to get worse for our Savior. How is it that we can be so indifferent at times to the cost of sin? How can we so often take for granted the greatness of His love?

*Holy Mary, Mother of God, pray for us sinners
now and at the hour of our death. Amen.*

*Glory be to the Father,
and to the Son, and to the Holy Spirit:
As it was in the beginning,
is now, and ever shall be, world without end. Amen*

*Oh my Jesus, forgive our sins and save us from the power of hell.
Lead all souls into heaven especially those
most in need of your mercy. Amen*

The Fifth Sorrowful Mystery
The Crucifixion

Hail Mary, full of grace, the Lord is with you; blessed are you among women, and blessed is the fruit of your womb, Jesus.

1) Who was crucified for my salvation. (P)

In this reflection we look at the big picture of Jesus' suffering. The mockery, the taunting, the humiliation, carrying His cross, being nailed to the cross, His death by asphyxiation are all part of it. Crucifixion was a barbaric, cruel, inhumane practice. And yet it was common place in the Roman Empire. This should certainly give us insight into how the Christian Faith transformed western civilization and the world.

So many secularists and atheists refuse to see how Jesus and His followers changed everything. In fact, they will argue that Christianity held the world back from development. And yet it is in what was formally known as Christendom that scientific and ethical advancements have taken hold. The teaching of the Bible that human beings are made in the image and likeness of God coupled with the teaching of Jesus that whatever we do to the least of our brothers and sisters we do unto Him; changed everything!

We only need to look at what happens when Christianity is ignored or discarded. Look at Hitler, Stalin, Mao, Pol Pot and others who headed atheist regimes and brought wholesale death and destruction. Without the teaching of the Bible there is no foundation for human dignity and human rights.

In our own nation as Christianity is more and more discarded we see the wholesale destruction of the unborn under the guise of "choice" as well as greater and greater exploitation of women by men. The safety of our senior citizens as they face health issues becomes more perilous by the day. In the book, *"The Hunger Games"* we see a future world where the destruction of innocent people is turned into a sport by the ruling elites and the general population. Without the teaching of Jesus and the Holy Bible we will be doomed to a new Roman Empire and all the barbarity that went with it. Jesus changes everything! The 80% of people in our country who claim to be Christians need to wake up to that fact before it is too late.

While the crucifixion was indeed barbaric, it once again points us to the unfathomable love of the Lord for each one of us. He endured what He did because He loves you and He loves me.

2) Who was nailed to the cross so that I might be forgiven.

We now turn to some of the individual components of crucifixion. His hands were nailed to a cross beam while His feet were nailed in such a way as to cause the most agony as the victim struggled to breath. Jesus, already severely weakened by an agonizing scourging would have had to struggle to lift His body to a more upright position in order to breath. Death would have been caused when the victim was no longer able to raise himself up and would then be suffocated as his lungs filled with fluids. This is certainly one more reminder of man's inhumanity to man when the teaching of our God is ignored.

3) Who prayed, "Father forgive them for they know not what they do."

A few years ago, the History Channel put out a series on the Bible. That series brilliantly captured this moment when Jesus prayed for His murderers. You can be certain the Roman soldiers who executed Jesus were used to being cursed by their victims. They would have been unfazed as the victims cursed them, their families, their lineage and posterity and wished upon them eternal damnation. But in the History Channels series we see a look of shock upon the faces of the soldiers as Jesus prays for them and those who plotted against Him. It was such a subtle scene as they are amazed at what they are hearing. A look of, "did I just hear that?" We can be certain that a man tortured and in total agony praying for those who did this to Him was something the soldiers had never heard before.

Jesus taught us to forgive those who hurt us, but He did not just teach it; He demonstrated it.

This also gives such great hope as we struggle with sin in our own lives. "Father forgive them, they know not what they do." Do any of us fully comprehend the enormity of sin? Do any of us realize the depths of love that would lead the Lord to embrace the cross so that we could be saved? How often we can take for granted that love. How often we can be indifferent to the price of our salvation. This prayer of Jesus should fill us with great hope as we struggle to overcome the sins of our own lives!

4) Who said to His Mother, "Woman, behold your son."

5) Who said to the beloved disciple, "behold your Mother."

Let's take a look at this passage from John's gospel chapter 19:26-27

When Jesus saw his mother and the disciple there whom he loved, he said to his mother, "Woman, behold, your son." Then he said to the disciple, "Behold, your mother." And from that hour the disciple took her into his home.

We already discussed at the Wedding Feast of Cana Jesus' use of the word "woman" when addressing His Mother. He is the new Adam and is proclaiming Mary to be the new Eve. The two times that Jesus uses the term woman in addressing His Mother are meant to be a contrast with what Eve did in the Garden of Eden. Eve encouraged Adam to sin. At the wedding Feast of Cana, the new Eve gets the new Adam to manifest His glory. In the Garden of Eden, the original woman participated in Adam's sin; as Jesus hangs on the cross the new "woman" supports Jesus as He is obedient unto death.

In the Garden of Eden, Adam names the woman Eve because she was to become the mother of all the living (Gen 3:20). Here Jesus gives His Mother to the "beloved disciple" to be his mother. The fact is we are all beloved disciples. John here is meant to represent all of us. So, on the cross Jesus gives us His Mother to be our Mother. Mary becomes the mother of all those born again in Christ.

We will see in the Glorious Mysteries how Jesus perfectly lives the 4th commandment of "Honor your father and mother." For now, it is important to recognize that we do not take away anything from Jesus when we imitate Him. Jesus honors His Mother, we are to do the same. We have a Mother in heaven who loves us and watches over us. We do not somehow give God greater honor if we choose to ignore this Mother in heaven.

We have pointed out in the past and will do so again now, God's plan of salvation is a family plan. Jesus came to unite us into the "Family of God." Certainly, a key person in almost every family is the mother. It would certainly be bizarre to think that Jesus gave us His Mother to be

173

our Mother and then expects us to for all practical purposes ignore her. And yet many Christians do for the most part ignore Our Lady. That cannot be what Jesus had in mind when He said, "Woman, behold your son...behold your mother."

6) Who said to the good thief, "today you will be with Me in paradise."

Let's take a look at this passage from Luke 23:39- 43:

> *Now one of the criminals hanging there reviled Jesus, saying, "Are you not the Messiah? Save yourself and us." The other, however, rebuking him, said in reply, "Have you no fear of God, for you are subject to the same condemnation? And indeed, we have been condemned justly, for the sentence we received corresponds to our crimes, but this man has done nothing criminal. Then he said, "Jesus, remember me when you come into your kingdom. He replied to him, "Amen, I say to you, today you will be with me in Paradise."*

There are a few important reflections on this passage. First of all Jesus is making it clear that His Kingdom has come. The man known as "the good thief" said "when you come into your kingdom...." Jesus in guaranteeing him paradise "today" implies that His kingdom has arrived.

Secondly, we see the incredible mercy of Jesus. The fact is in this life it is never too late to come to saving faith. It is never too late to repent of our sins. This man recognizes that he is guilty of serious crimes and he asks for mercy. We could say that he went to confession on the cross. And on the cross Jesus gave him complete forgiveness. Catholic theology would call this a "plenary indulgence."

174

As a priest I have had the great privilege of being with people as they are facing death who humbly confess their sins and receive God's saving grace at the end of their lives. I sadly have also encountered people who either refuse to take responsibility for their sins or who refuse to trust that God could have mercy on them. The mercy received by the "good thief" should be a sign of hope for all of us and our loved ones that it is never too late **in this life** to receive the mercy of God!

7) Who prayed, "My God, My God, why have you forsaken Me."

This is probably one of the most misunderstood lines in all of scripture. There are actually people who believe that Jesus despaired, lost faith and died. Nothing could be further from the truth! When we understand the Old Testament and how it is the foundation of the New we see Jesus is proclaiming victory and the faithfulness of the Father. Without knowing the Old Testament, we would get the total opposite idea.

Jesus here is quoting psalm 22. Psalm 22 was part of what was known as a "Todah Liturgy" (Todah is translated into English as thanksgiving. The Greek word for thanksgiving is eucharist) In a Todah Liturgy a person would make a sacrifice to God of bread and wine when the Lord had delivered them from what had appeared to be a hopeless situation. The psalm starts with what appears to be a hopeless cry of despair, but it goes on to speak of the faithfulness of God. In fact, psalm 22 is a prophetic psalm that points us to the saving work of Jesus and how He would triumph over death and His saving Word would go to the ends of the earth. Let's take a look at this psalm (I will highlight some of the passages that most point us to Jesus and His triumph):

175

My God, my God, why have you abandoned me?
Why so far from my call for help,
from my cries of anguish?
My God, I call by day, but you do not answer;
by night, but I have no relief.
Yet you are enthroned as the Holy One;
you are the glory of Israel.
In you our fathers trusted;
they trusted and you rescued them.
To you they cried out and they escaped;
in you they trusted and were not disappointed.
But I am a worm, not a man,
scorned by men, despised by the people.
All who see me mock me;
they curl their lips and jeer;
they shake their heads at me:
"He relied on the LORD—let him deliver him;
if he loves him, let him rescue him."
For you drew me forth from the womb,
made me safe at my mother's breasts.
Upon you I was thrust from the womb;
since my mother bore me you are my God.
Do not stay far from me,
for trouble is near,
and there is no one to help.
Many bulls surround me;
fierce bulls of Bashan encircle me.

They open their mouths against me,
lions that rend and roar.
Like water my life drains away;
all my bones are disjointed.
My heart has become like wax,
it melts away within me.
As dry as a potsherd is my throat;
my tongue cleaves to my palate;
you lay me in the dust of death.
Dogs surround me;
a pack of evildoers closes in on me.
They have pierced my hands and my feet
I can count all my bones.
They stare at me and gloat;
they divide my garments among them;
for my clothing they cast lots.
But you, LORD, do not stay far off;
my strength, come quickly to help me.
Deliver my soul from the sword,
my life from the grip of the dog.
Save me from the lion's mouth,
my poor life from the horns of wild bulls.

Then I will proclaim your name to my brethren;
in the assembly I will praise you:
"You who fear the LORD, give praise
All descendants of Jacob, give honor;

177

show reverence, all descendants of Israel!
For he has not spurned or disdained
the misery of this poor wretch,
Did not turn away from me,
but heard me when I cried out.
I will offer praise in the great assembly;
my vows I will fulfill before those who fear him.
The poor will eat their fill;
those who seek the LORD will offer praise. May your hearts enjoy
life forever!"
All the ends of the earth
will remember and turn to the LORD;
All the families of nations
will bow low before him.
For kingship belongs to the LORD,
the ruler over the nations.
All who sleep in the earth
will bow low before God;
All who have gone down into the dust
will kneel in homage.
And I will live for the LORD;
my descendants will serve you.
The generation to come will be told of the Lord,
that they may proclaim to a people yet unborn
the deliverance you have brought.

This psalm certainly points us to the saving work of Jesus. It predicts the mockery of people saying He trusted in the Lord, let the Lord

178

deliver Him. It speaks of His hands and feet being pierced to His being saved from lasting death and His saving work being proclaimed to the ends of the earth. Notice the one praying the psalm will be spared, He will be in the great assembly, His deliverance will be proclaimed generation after generation. Jesus on the cross is proclaiming the faithfulness of the Father and His own victory.

This psalm also points us to the Holy Eucharist. The last Supper was Jesus' "Todah Liturgy." It is interesting to note that the ancient rabbis had predicted that in the Messianic age that all sacrifices would cease, except for the Todah. That teaching is lived out every day as the Church offers the Todah of Jesus, the Holy sacrifice of the Mass.

That's a lot to get across in one little line. But when we understand how the OT is the foundation of the New, when we choose to see the connections between the two, we get a whole different understanding then when we superficially read the words of the NT.

8) Who prayed, "It is Finished."

We have been following a thread since the Last Supper to help us comprehend this often-misunderstood prayer of the Lord. We need to examine what was the "it" that was finished? Some Christians argue that Jesus is speaking of the work of salvation. They speak of "the finished work of Christ." They say Jesus did it all on the cross and there is nothing left to do.

But it just takes a moment to realize that Jesus was not speaking of the work of salvation. After all he had not yet risen from the dead and that was a real important aspect of His saving work! He had not yet ascended into heaven, He had not yet sent the Holy Spirit. All of those are essential aspects of the work of salvation!

179

To understand the "it" that was finished we need to delve into the structure of the Passover meal. The Passover was centered on four cups of wine. We have already seen how Jesus gave us the Eucharist at the third cup. We have also seen that after singing the "great hallel" that Jesus rather than going to the 4th cup (which is what normally would happen), went instead out to a garden. In the garden He prayed, "Father, let this cup pass...." Let's once again take a look at the Last Supper as it appears in Mark 14:22-26:

> *While they were eating, he took bread, said the blessing, broke it, and gave it to them, and said, "Take it; this is my body." Then he took a cup, gave thanks, and gave it to them, and they all drank from it. He said to them, "This is my blood of the covenant, which will be shed for many. Amen, I say to you, I shall not drink again the fruit of the vine until the day when I drink it new in the kingdom of God." Then, after singing a hymn, they went out to the Mount of Olives.*

Notice how Jesus says He will not drink again from the fruit of the vine until He drinks it in the Kingdom of God. But Jesus drinks some sour wine on the cross. Either Jesus was wrong, or He entered His Kingdom on the cross—which is what He did.

Let's now take a look at what Jesus does on the cross as it appears in John 19:28-30:

> *After this, aware that everything was now finished, in order that the scripture might be fulfilled, Jesus said, "I thirst." There was a vessel filled with common wine. So they put a sponge soaked in wine on a sprig of hyssop and put it up to his mouth. When Jesus had taken the wine, he said, "It is finished." And bowing his head, he handed over the spirit.*

180

This, first, occurs right after Jesus gave His Mother to the beloved disciple to be his mother. It is certainly implied here that making His mother the mother of all beloved disciples was an important aspect of what He needed to accomplish.

Secondly, notice that He was given the wine on a hyssop branch. A hyssop branch was the kind of branch that was to be used in putting the blood of the lamb on the doorpost and lintel at the first Passover when God was to free His people from slavery. John includes this detail to highlight how Jesus has now fulfilled the expectations of the Jewish people in giving us a new Passover.

And finally, and most importantly for our purposes here, we see that the "it" that was finished was the Last Supper. The Last Supper and Calvary are one saving event; two acts of one play as it were. Jesus consumes the 4th cup, the cup of consummation on the cross. It is the Last Supper that transforms a Roman execution into a saving sacrifice (see Scott Hahn's, *"Consuming the Word,"*).

This is why St. Paul in 1 Cor 11:26 declares, *"For as often as you eat this bread and drink the cup, you proclaim the death of the Lord until he comes."* Calvary began at the Last Supper. The last Supper was finished on Calvary. Whenever we come to Mass we proclaim the death (and resurrection) of the Lord. We not only proclaim it, we participate in the once and for all sacrifice of Jesus.

How is that? For the ancient Jewish people, whenever they participated in Passover they considered themselves at the original event. They believed that the saving work of God transcended time and space. St. Paul is making the same point. Whenever we participate in the "New Passover" we are present at the original event. The saving work of Jesus cannot be limited to one time or place—it transcends all

181

of human history. Jesus is God and God transcends time. Every time we come to Mass we plug into that once and for all saving work of our Savior; we are at the Last Supper, we are at Calvary with Mary, we are at the empty tomb. In declaring "It is finished" Jesus was speaking volumes.

9) The new Adam whose side was opened and water, symbolizing baptism; and blood, symbolizing the Holy Eucharist, flowed from the Temple of His body, forming His Bride.

Once again to understand the saving work of Jesus we need to see how He fulfills the OT. Again, we see the parallels between the Creation and the Fall and the work of our salvation. The NT portrays Jesus as the new Adam and the Church as His bride. We need to go to Genesis to learn about the bride of the original Adam. We read in Genesis 2: 20-24:

> *The man gave names to all the tame animals, all the birds of the air, and all the wild animals; but none proved to be a helper suited to the man. So the LORD God cast a deep sleep on the man, and while he was asleep, he took out one of his ribs and closed up its place with flesh. The LORD God then built the rib that he had taken from the man into a woman. When he brought her to the man, the man said: "This one, at last, is bone of my bones and flesh of my flesh; This one shall be called 'woman,' for out of man this one has been taken." That is why a man leaves his father and mother and clings to his wife, and the two of them become one body.*

Adam's bride was formed from his side when he was in a deep sleep. In John's gospel we see the bride of Jesus, the Holy Church, formed

182

from His side as He is in the sleep of death on the cross. Let's take a look at John 19: 31-36:

> *Now since it was preparation day, in order that the bodies might not remain on the cross on the Sabbath, for the Sabbath day of that week was a solemn one, the Jews asked Pilate that their legs be broken, and they be taken down. So the soldiers came and broke the legs of the first and then of the other one who was crucified with Jesus. But when they came to Jesus and saw that he was already dead, they did not break his legs, but one soldier thrust his lance into his side, and immediately blood and water flowed out. An eyewitness has testified, and his testimony is true; he knows that he is speaking the truth, so that you also may [come to] believe. For this happened so that the scripture passage might be fulfilled*

Notice this occurs so that scripture might be fulfilled. How is scripture fulfilled? Again, we need to understand the parallels between Creation and salvation (the new creation) if we are to understand what St. John is trying to get across to us. You will notice in vs 35 John gets all excited that an eyewitness is testifying to this. Why is John all excited? Because John knows that Jesus is the new Adam. He sees in this the creation of Jesus' bride, the Holy Church. The water symbolizes baptism and the blood the Holy Eucharist; the two primary sacraments that form us into the Church.

In the reflection we said how water and blood flowed "from the Temple of His body." This is to remind us of another passage which was pointing to Jesus and how the sacraments, especially of baptism and the Holy Eucharist were going to change the world. We read in the prophet Ezekiel 47:1-12:

183

Then he brought me back to the entrance of the temple, and there! I saw water flowing out from under the threshold of the temple toward the east, for the front of the temple faced east. The water flowed out toward the right side of the temple to the south of the altar. He brought me by way of the north gate and around the outside to the outer gate facing east; there I saw water trickling from the southern side. When he continued eastward with a measuring cord in his hand, he measured off a thousand cubits and had me wade through the water; it was ankle-deep. He measured off another thousand cubits and once more had me wade through the water; it was up to the knees. He measured another thousand cubits and had me wade through the water; it was up to my waist. Once more he measured off a thousand cubits. Now it was a river I could not wade across. The water had risen so high, I would have to swim—a river that was impassable. Then he asked me, "Do you see this, son of man?" He brought me to the bank of the river and had me sit down. As I was returning, I saw along the bank of the river a great many trees on each side. He said to me, "This water flows out into the eastern district, runs down into the Arabah and empties into the polluted waters of the sea to freshen them. Wherever it flows, the river teems with every kind of living creature; fish will abound. Where these waters flow they refresh; everything lives where the river goes. Fishermen will stand along its shore from En-gedi to En-eglaim; it will become a place for drying nets, and it will abound with as many kinds of fish as the Great Sea. Its marshes and swamps shall not be made fresh, but will be left for salt. Along each bank of the river every kind of fruit tree will grow; their leaves will not wither, nor will their fruit fail. Every month they will bear fresh fruit because the waters of the

184

river flow out from the sanctuary. Their fruit is used for food, and their leaves for healing."

In this section of Ezekiel, he is looking forward to a new Israel. And what leads to the new Israel is a saving stream flowing from the Temple. Well Jesus told us in John 2:19-21 that the Temple was pointing to him. In other words, the Temple was a type of Christ. Ezekiel sees a saving stream flowing from the Temple bringing healing and life. In vs 8 we are told this saving stream goes to the sea and makes salt water fresh. Well for the ancient Jews the sea was a sign of the pagan way of life. Salt water kills and cannot give life to people. But in this passage the saving stream from the sanctuary will make the salt waters fresh. This is a reference to how the Gentile people will be transformed by the sacraments and become the children of God. Ezekiel 47 begins to be fulfilled as Jesus hangs on the cross, but its fulfillment continues as the bride of Christ brings God's saving grace to the world.

10) Whose Mother held the lifeless Body of her Son in her arms. (P)

As I explained in the introduction I had very little devotion to the Blessed Mother in my early life. In the seminary and my early priesthood, I saw Mary as an "ecumenical problem" and thought that in paying scant attention to her I was helping to overcome the divisions among Christians. A dying 17-year-old boy and his mother changed all that for me! Seeing Joyce Bates sit at her son's bedside, powerless to help him, made Mary come alive for me. I finally got it!

If our suffering is redemptive as St. Paul so clearly teaches in Colossians 1:24. If our suffering is an essential aspect of salvation as Paul teaches in Rom 8:16-39 and St. Peter clearly teaches in 1 Peter

4:12-13; then Mary's suffering was certainly an essential aspect of the work of salvation. If we are called to suffer with Jesus, there can be no doubt that no one has suffered with Jesus the way Mary did! There is no greater pain than a loving parent losing a child. To see her Son treated in such a deplorable fashion had to be pain for her beyond all understanding. Mary shared in the suffering of her Son in a way that is beyond words to explain. Only a parent who has lost a child can begin to understand her agony!

Holy Mary, Mother of God, pray for us sinners
now and at the hour of our death. Amen.

Glory be to the Father,
and to the Son, and to the Holy Spirit:
As it was in the beginning,
is now, and ever shall be, world without end. Amen

Oh my Jesus, forgive our sins and save us from the power of hell.
Lead all souls into heaven especially those
most in need of your mercy. Amen

Section 4

The

Glorious

Mysteries

The First Glorious Mystery
The Resurrection

Hail Mary, full of grace, the Lord is with you; blessed are you among women, and blessed is the fruit of your womb, **Jesus***:*

1) Who conquered sin and death on the day of the Resurrection. (P)

Since the day sin first came into the world, death has been humanities greatest fear. When we look at the book of Genesis we see that it did not take long for sin to lead to death as we are told the story of Cain and Abel (Genesis 4:1-16). But in the Garden God had promised a Savior even as our first parents had turned away from the Lord. Genesis 3:15 is known in Catholic theology as the "proto-evangelium" (the first gospel). God promised, "*I will put enmity between you and the woman, and between your offspring and hers; they will strike at your head, while you strike at their heel.*"

Mary, of course, is the "woman" spoken of here in that her Son crushed the head of the serpent at a place called Golgotha, which means "the place of the skull." In the NAB the one word is translated as "offspring," but a more literal translation would be "seed.' The Greek word here is "spermatosa" which is normally associated with a man. Jesus is the only person in history who could be considered "the seed of the woman" since He had no human father.

Death came into the world as a result of sin. The following passages teach that clearly:

Romans 5:12-21   Death comes from sin

188

Genesis 2:15	God warns Adam if he eats the forbidden fruit he will die
Genesis 3:2	Eve tells the serpent she cannot eat the fruit or she will die
Wisdom 1:13 & 2:23-24	God did not make death
1 Corinthians 15:22	All die in Adam; all will be brought to life in Christ

Jesus took death on and overcame it on the day of the Resurrection. Because of Him death can no longer hold us. Those who put their faith in Jesus will share His Resurrection.

It is necessary to note that bodily resurrection is an essential aspect of our faith. The fact is, the human soul never ceases to exist. Death is the separation of soul from the body. Jesus did not have to rise from the dead to assure the continued existence of the soul. He rose from the dead in his body so that we could eventually be brought body and soul to heaven.

Since sin is the cause of death an essential aspect of our faith is that we strive to conquer the sins of our lives. As we reflected in the Sorrowful Mysteries Jesus forms His bride (the Church) through the sacraments, especially Baptism and the Eucharist. The graces these sacraments afford us is meant to empower us to share in the life of Jesus. Jesus of course, never sinned. Those who are now members of His body are called with His grace to conquer sin in our lives. Through faith in him we share in His life and His victory. Death and sin are no longer to rule us.

189

2) Who rose from the dead on the third day in fulfillment of scripture.

The NT tells us that Jesus rose from the dead on the third day in fulfillment of scripture; the problem with that teaching is that there is scant evidence of that in the OT. Nowhere does the OT explicitly say that the Messiah will die and on the third day be raised from the dead. Some will point to Hos 6:2, *"He will revive us after two days; on the third day he will raise us up, to live in his presence."* Others look to Psalm 16:10, *"For you will not abandon my soul to Sheol, nor let your devout one see the pit. You will show me the path to life, abounding joy in your presence, the delights at your right hand forever."*

The trouble with the Hosea passage is that no NT writer cites it as an example of the Resurrection and the second one says nothing about the third day. What is going on here? Were the NT writers trying to pull a fast one? Of course not!

The biblical writers are relying on typology. There are two people in particular that NT writers are referring to when it says Jesus rose on the third day in fulfillment of scripture. The first person is Isaac, the second is Jonah.

Let's take a look at the story of Isaac and Abraham from Genesis 22:1-14:

> *Sometime afterward, God put Abraham to the test and said to him: Abraham! "Here I am!" he replied. Then God said: Take your son Isaac, your only one, whom you love, and go to the land of Moriah. There offer him up as a burnt offering on one of the heights that I will point out to you. Early the next morning Abraham saddled his donkey, took with him two of his*

servants and his son Isaac, and after cutting the wood for the burnt offering, set out for the place of which God had told him.

On the third day Abraham caught sight of the place from a distance. Abraham said to his servants: "Stay here with the donkey, while the boy and I go on over there. We will worship and then come back to you." So Abraham took the wood for the burnt offering and laid it on his son Isaac, while he himself carried the fire and the knife. As the two walked on together, Isaac spoke to his father Abraham. "Father!" he said. "Here I am," he replied. Isaac continued, "Here are the fire and the wood, but where is the sheep for the burnt offering?" "My son," Abraham answered, "God will provide the sheep for the burnt offering." Then the two walked on together.

When they came to the place of which God had told him, Abraham built an altar there and arranged the wood on it. **Next he bound**[*] **his son Isaac, and put him on top of the wood on the altar.** *Then Abraham reached out and took the knife to slaughter his son. But the angel of the LORD called to him from heaven, "Abraham, Abraham!" "Here I am," he answered. "Do not lay your hand on the boy," said the angel. "Do not do the least thing to him. For now I know that you fear God, since you did not withhold from me your son, your only one." Abraham looked up and saw a single ram caught by its horns in the thicket. So Abraham went and took the ram and offered it up as a burnt offering in place of his son. Abraham named that place Yahweh-yireh;* **hence people today say, "On the mountain the LORD will provide."**

There are many parallels with this story and the saving work of our Lord. First, we have a loving father who is willing to sacrifice his son

191

for the salvation of the world. And while Abraham consents, God does not actually make him sacrifice his son. This contrasts with God the Father who does allow His Son to be sacrificed for the salvation of the world

Secondly, many theologians have pointed out how Abraham was a very old man at this point while Isaac was in the prime of life. The only way the sacrifice could have been successful was if Isaac freely cooperated. This certainly corresponds with the saving work of Jesus who freely consented to the crucifixion for the salvation of the world.

Third, Isaac here carries the wood for the sacrifice just as Jesus carried the wood of the cross.

Fourth, Isaac says to his father, "Here is the wood and the fire but where is the lamb (translated above as sheep) for the sacrifice? Abraham responds, "God will provide the lamb." This, interestingly enough, occurs at a mountain range called Moriah. One of the peaks of that range is a place called Calvary. We also learn from the psalms that the phrase for "God will provide" (Yahweh-jireh) was prefixed to the name of the town where this occurs. The town was originally known as Salem but later becomes Jerusalem. It is of course in Jerusalem that God does provide the lamb of sacrifice to take away the sins of the world.

However, what is most important here, is the fact that for three days Isaac was as good as dead in the eyes of his father, but on the third day he is restored to Abraham.

Through this story of Abraham and Isaac God was pointing us to the saving work of the Lord.

The 2nd type of Jesus that points us to the resurrection is the story of Jonah. Jesus Himself tells us that the story of Jonah was pointing us to the Resurrection when He says in Matthew 12:39-41:

> *He said to them in reply, "An evil and unfaithful generation seeks a sing, but no sign will be given it except the sign of Jonah the prophet. Just as Jonah was in the belly of the whale three days and three nights, so will the Son of Man be in the heart of the earth three days and three nights. At the judgment, the men of Nineveh will arise with this generations and condemn it, because they repented at the preaching of Jonah; and there is something greater than Jonah here.*

The truth is, without typology there is no way we can say that the Resurrection on the third day fulfilled scripture. But with typology we see Christ's Resurrection prefigured in the lives of two of the heroes of the OT.

3) Who rose from the dead on the 8th day; Sunday, the first day of the week to demonstrate that there is a new creation.

We already saw in the 4th Joyful Mystery how God was preparing His people for a new creation by commanding that all the males born to the Israelites were to be circumcised on the 8th day. Also, in the major feasts of the OT the 8th day celebration was often more important than the 1st day. In these ways God was pointing to a new creation. In the Bible creation took place in 7 days. The 8th day is the beginning of a new week symbolizing a new creation.

So in the OT their holy day was Saturday, the end of the week, but ours is now Sunday. Why? Because for the Jews their redemption would come after centuries of waiting. For us, before we do one thing,

Jesus has already won the victory. We are part of the new creation where Jesus has already conquered sin and death.

There are groups, such as the 7th day Adventist who follow Christ, but who refuse to see how Jesus has transformed the holy day of the week from the Sabbath (Saturday) into "the Lord's Day" (Sunday). Jesus of course rose on a Sunday. Every occurrence where He appears to His followers, when the day is mentioned it is Sunday. All through salvation history God was pointing us to the triumph of Jesus on the 8th day, Sunday. From the very beginning of Christianity, we see the first Jewish Christians going to the Temple on the Sabbath, but joining with their Christian brothers and sisters on Sunday, the Lord's Day.

If you are anything like me, you have probably wondered about this idea of a "new creation." I know for years I harbored doubts about how much of a new creation it was. After all that had happened following the Resurrection, the Romans still ruled the world in brutal fashion; the Christians experienced horrendous persecution, the world was still filled with sin and death—where was the new creation? In many ways it looked like the same old creation to me.

But we can learn here from both science and the scriptures. In the Bible the original creation did not happen all at once. Creation unfolded slowly. After all, the sun, moon and stars only came on the 4th day. The animal world and the human race only appeared on the 6th day. The world of science tells us that the original creation of the earth and the human race unfolded over billions of years. Scientists tell us that carbon (a necessary ingredient for life) did not exist when the universe was created. Carbon comes from exploding stars. Part of the creation of life was dependent on stars not only forming, but then growing old and exploding spewing carbon into the universe. Part of our DNA as humans is stardust. Needless to say, science tells us the original creation of human beings happened very, very, very slowly. Why should we expect the new creation to be any different?

As the saving message of Jesus spread through the world, the world was changed; slowly, over time, but transformed nonetheless! Much of the pagan world was filled with hopelessness and despair; Jesus changed all that! Jesus brought meaning and purpose to life. He brought the sense of the dignity of every person no matter what their state in life. He assured people that the all-powerful God loved the weak and lowly and would raise them up. In the words of our Blessed Mother, He would, "cast down the mighty from their thrones and lift up the lowly." Jesus changed everything! Slowly, over time Jesus and His life-giving gospel transformed the face of the earth.

4) Who appeared to Mary Magdalene on the day of the Resurrection.

This reflection gives us the opportunity to see how Jesus transforms the face of the earth. In Jewish culture back then, women were not permitted to be witnesses in any legal proceedings. Certainly, in the Muslim world today women are not recognized as equal partners to men. But Jesus chose to allow a woman to be the very first witness to the most momentous event in human history.

We have already seen in Genesis how at the creation of the woman that Adam did not strictly give her a name, he shared his with her. He was man, she was woman. It was only after sin came into the world that Adam gives her a name showing dominion over her. But before sin, there was equality (different roles, but equal). In appearing to Mary Magdalene first Jesus is showing that His saving work restores the original equal dignity of men and women. This is the first evidence of the new creation.

5) Who appeared to His Blessed Mother in a garden.

Some of you may be thinking, "hold on there, Father, where's that in the Bible?" The answer is that it is not in the Bible, it comes to us through tradition. Before we examine this let me share a story with you.

I was in my first assignment as a priest. A woman came to me who was very upset. With tears in her eyes she told me of how her daughter lives in Florida and she rarely gets a chance to see her. She burst into sobs when she told me of how her daughter had come back to Cleveland for some event and never came to see her (the mother). This woman was heartbroken that her daughter could not bother to take the time to see her while she was in town. Most reasonable people would agree with this woman that her daughter was pretty thoughtless in this situation and caused her mother incredible heartache. We might even say the daughter was clueless as to good manners and respect for her mother

Let's look at the days before the Resurrection of the Lord. His most trusted Apostle denied that he even knew who Jesus was. His other Apostles abandoned Him in His hour of need. He suffered incredible torture and humiliation, but He was not alone. His Mother met Him as He carried the cross. His Mother stood at the foot of the cross powerless to take away her Son's agony. After His death His Mother held His lifeless body in her arms. Is there anyone who believes that Jesus would be so clueless and heartless and thoughtless as to fail to come to His Mother after the Resurrection?

In the Church of the Holy Sepulcher in Jerusalem there is a chapel that is said to be built over the garden where Jesus appeared to his mother after the Resurrection. Since the original Adam and Eve brought defeat

196

to the human race in a garden, it was only appropriate that the new Adam and the new Eve would be reunited to celebrate the victory of the human race in a garden.

6) **Who opened the scriptures to the disciples on the road to Emmaus.**

7) **Whose disciples recognized Him in the "breaking of the bread."**

Here we begin to get to some of the most important aspects of our faith when it comes to how His people will encounter Jesus in their lives. On the first day of the resurrection Jesus and the gospel writers point us to the Holy Mass. There are four aspects of the Mass, two minor and two major and all of them are seen in the journey to Emmaus.

The Life Teen movement describes the four aspects of the Mass as 1) the gather, 2) the proclaim, 3) the break and 4) the send. Let's take a look at this passage from Luke 24:13-35, and examine how it is pointing us to the Mass:

> *Now that very day two of them were going to a village seven miles from Jerusalem called Emmaus, and they were conversing about all the things that had occurred. And it happened that while they were conversing and debating, Jesus himself drew near and walked with them,* **but their eyes were prevented from recognizing him.** *He asked them, "What are you discussing as you walk along?" They stopped, looking downcast. One of them, named Cleopas, said to him in reply, "Are you the only visitor to Jerusalem who does not know of the things that have taken place there in these days?" And he replied to them, "What sort of*

197

things?" They said to him, "The things that happened to Jesus the Nazarene, who was a prophet mighty in deed and word before God and all the people, how our chief priests and rulers both handed him over to a sentence of death and crucified him. But we were hoping that he would be the one to redeem Israel; and besides all this, it is now the third day since this took place. Some women from our group, however, have astounded us: they were at the tomb early in the morning and did not find his body; they came back and reported that they had indeed seen a vision of angels who announced that he was alive. Then some of those with us went to the tomb and found things just as the women had described, but him they did not see." And he said to them, "Oh, how foolish you are! How slow of heart to believe all that the prophets spoke! Was it not necessary that the Messiah should suffer these things and enter into his glory?" Then beginning with Moses and all the prophets, he interpreted to them what referred to him in all the scriptures. As they approached the village to which they were going, he gave the impression that he was going on farther. But they urged him, "Stay with us, for it is nearly evening and the day is almost over." So he went in to stay with them. And it happened that, while he was with them at table, he took bread, said the blessing, broke it, and gave it to them. With that their eyes were opened and they recognized him, but he vanished from their sight. Then they said to each other, "Were not our hearts burning [within us] while he spoke to us on the way and opened the scriptures to us?" So they set out at once and returned to Jerusalem where they found gathered together the eleven and those with them who were saying, "The Lord has truly been raised and has appeared to Simon!" Then the two

recounted what had taken place on the way and how he was
made known to them in the breaking of the bread.

In this we see the four aspects of the Mass. First the gather as Jesus approached the disciples and walked with them on the journey. Second the proclaim as Jesus "opens the scriptures to them." Third the break as the disciples recognize Jesus in the breaking of the bread. And finally, the send as the disciples rush off to tell the good news that they have encountered the risen Lord.

The two primary aspects of the Mass that our reflections focus on are "the proclaim" and "the break."

First, the proclaim. In every Mass we open the scriptures to those who are present. In every Mass there is a proclamation of a psalm and a gospel. In most Sunday Masses we hear from the OT and another NT reading that is not a gospel. Many of the prayers of the Mass come right from the scriptures. On the journey to Emmaus Jesus opens the scriptures to the disciples. We are told that their hearts were burning within them as He opened the scriptures. It is also important to note that what Jesus told them about scripture is not recorded in the Bible. That teaching where the disciple's hearts were burning inside them has come down to us through the Tradition of the Church.

The second reflection above says that the disciples recognized Jesus in "the breaking of the bread." This was the phrase the first Christians used for the celebration of the Eucharist. At Emmaus we see Jesus use the same fourfold movement that was used in the miracle of the multiplication of the loaves and at the Last Supper. Jesus takes, blesses, breaks and then gave the bread to the disciples. With that fourfold movement their eyes are opened to recognize the Lord.

St. Luke in recalling this story for us is pointing to how we can now encounter the risen Lord every time we gather for the Mass. At every Mass the scriptures are opened, and we recognize Jesus in the "breaking of the bread."

8) Who said to the Apostles "peace be with you."

Let's take a look at this passage in John 20: 19-23 from which this and the next reflection will be drawn:

> *On the evening of that first day of the week, when the doors were locked, where the disciples were, for fear of the Jews, Jesus came and stood in their midst and said to them, "Peace be with you." When he had said this, he showed them his hands and his side. The disciples rejoiced when they saw the Lord. [Jesus] said to them again, "Peace be with you. As the Father has sent me, so I send you." And when he had said this, he breathed on them and said to them, "Receive the Holy Spirit. Whose sins you forgive are forgiven them, and whose sins you retain are retained."*

This reflection helps me realize how far I still must go if I am to follow the example of the Lord in my dealings with others. Had Jesus been like me He would have said when He appeared to the Apostles something like, "Hey Peter, so you don't know who I am huh?" Or "Hey guys, thanks for being there when I needed you—thanks for nothing!" But that is not what Jesus said. He said, "Peace be with you." He chose to build up the Apostles rather than tearing them down. He chose words of love rather than sarcasm. Often my first reaction to situations where I have been hurt is to want to get even, strike out, make them pay. That is not what the Lord calls us to. The world would certainly be a much better place if we all followed Jesus' example of love, mercy and kindness. Reflecting on His words of "peace be with you" can help us all to become better people.

9) Who breathed on the Apostles saying, "Receive the Holy Spirit, whose sins you forgive are forgiven them, whose sins you retain are retained."

Here we have Jesus giving to His Church the sacrament of Reconciliation (Confession). Jesus says in vs 21, "As the father has sent Me, so I send you." The fact is that the Father sent Jesus to forgive sins; Jesus is now commissioning the Apostles to do the same.

This is only the second time in the Bible when God breathes on people (the first was when God breathed life into Adam in Genesis). He is clearly giving them the power to forgive sins and to retain them. So the question is, "how could they know which sins of a person to forgive and which to retain if they do not know the sins?" This commission that Jesus gives the Apostles implies that people would need to confess their sins, otherwise how could they know which sins to forgive and which to retain?

Throughout the Bible we see God looking for people to take responsibility for their sins. If they take responsibility God forgives them. In the story of Adam and Eve God asks them why they were hiding. God of course knew why they were hiding, He wanted them to fall on their knees and confess, but they did not—Adam instead blames "the woman." In the story of Cain and Abel God asks Cain where his brother was; and Cain responds, 'am I my brother's keeper?" God knew what happened to Abel so why did He ask Cain about his brother? Because God was looking for a confession. In the story of David and Bathsheba and the death of her husband Uriah the Hittite we see David take responsibility for his sin and God forgives him, although there are consequences (see 2 Samuel 12:1-13). Throughout the Bible we see God's desire for people to take responsibility for their sins and then they receive forgiveness. We also see people refuse to take responsibility (Adam and Cain) and their sins have dire consequences. In the sacrament of reconciliation our merciful God gives us the opportunity to take responsibility for our sins so that we might receive His mercy.

Some people try to explain this passage away by arguing that what Jesus was really saying was, "when you preach the gospel and people come to faith they will then be forgiven. If you preach the gospel and people refuse to come to faith their sins will be retained." That of course is not at all what Jesus said here. He gave the power to forgive sins to the first priests of His Church.

In giving this incredible power to His Church Jesus wants us to know how much we need each other. As we have seen earlier in this book many people today try to take a very individualistic approach to faith; a "me and Jesus" attitude. But Jesus wants us to realize how much we need the community of faith. He gave us the sacrament of Reconciliation, so we can humbly come to His Church, take responsibility for our sins, and receive His astounding mercy.

10) The Good Shepherd who entrusted the shepherd's staff to Peter. (P)

Let's take a look at this passage from John 21:15-19:

> *When they had finished breakfast, Jesus said to Simon Peter, "Simon, son of John, do you love me more than these?" He said to him, "Yes, Lord, you know that I love you." He said to him, "Feed my lambs." He then said to him a second time,*

202

"Simon, son of John, do you love me?" He said to him, "Yes, Lord, you know that I love you." He said to him, "Tend my sheep." He said to him the third time, "Simon, son of John, do you love me?" Peter was distressed that he had said to him a third time, "Do you love me?" and he said to him, "Lord, you know everything; you know that I love you." [Jesus] said to him, "Feed my sheep. Amen, amen, I say to you, when you were younger, you used to dress yourself and go where you wanted; but when you grow old, you will stretch out your hands, and someone else will dress you and lead you where you do not want to go." He said this signifying by what kind of death he would glorify God. And when he had said this, he said to him, "Follow me."

The question of authority is a huge issue if we are to know, love and serve our God. Why is that? How are we to know God if we have no source to turn to which can with assurance tell us who God is? After all how can we know the Bible is God's Word unless some authority can with absolute certainty tell us, "these books are God's Word and these other books are not"? How can we know what moral precepts God expects us to obey if we have no sure source that can say, "these are the commands of God?" Without authority we can only "think" or "feel" or "have a personal opinion"—*we cannot know.*

In this and the next two mysteries we will deal with the issue of authority. As Catholics we believe that God has established an authority on earth that can speak infallibly in His Name. That authority is His holy Catholic Church led by the Vicar of Christ, the pope. We have already seen in the third Luminous mystery how God renamed Simon "Rock" (or Peter).

In the third Luminous Mystery we discussed how Jesus gave to Peter the "keys of the Kingdom." We pointed out how the image of the "key" came from Isaiah 22:21-22 and symbolized the office of prime minister in the kingdom of David. We saw how Isaiah 22 occurred 500 years after King David and stressed that the keys symbolized an office with succession. Jesus of course, is the King in the line of David and so in giving the keys to Peter He was establishing an office in His Kingdom on earth, the holy Church.

Each gospel writer makes the point of Peter's authority in a different way. In Matthew 16 Jesus renames Simon, giving him the name of Peter and gives him the keys of the Kingdom. In Luke Jesus at the Last Supper says to Peter that after he (Peter) has repented of his denial and turned back to Jesus, that Jesus will pray that his (Peter's) faith will never fail (Luke 22:31-32). Here in John's gospel we see Jesus rename Peter the first time He meets him (John 1:42) and here (John 21:15-19) He entrusts the shepherd's staff to Peter.

If Jesus is the "Good Shepherd" why does He tell Peter to feed His sheep? Because the Lord is ascending to heaven and has entrusted His own authority to His Church. Jesus here is giving Peter the task of shepherding His flock. A shepherd obviously has great authority over the flock. A good shepherd would never let the sheep wander on their own, the shepherd needs to guide, protect, watch over and care for the sheep.

As we continue through the Mysteries of the rosary we will follow a thread on the issue of authority as well as examining other issues.

Holy Mary, Mother of God, pray for us sinners
now and at the hour of our death. Amen.

Glory be to the Father,
and to the Son, and to the Holy Spirit:
As it was in the beginning,
is now, and ever shall be, world without end. Amen

Oh my Jesus, forgive our sins and save us from the power of hell.
Lead all souls into heaven especially those
most in need of your mercy. Amen

The Second Glorious Mystery
The Ascension into Heaven

Hail Mary, full of grace, the Lord is with you; blessed are you among women, and blessed is the fruit of your womb, Jesus.

1) Who ascended into heaven to prepare a place for me. (P)

Our greatest hope on earth is to have eternal life with our Savior in the glory of heaven. As one wise man once put it, "We're only here to get out of here." This world and everything in this world is passing away. At the heart of our faith is the promise that we will not only go to heaven, but that we will share in the glory of our Lord. We will see in the last two mysteries of the rosary (the Assumption and the Coronation of Mary) how a part of the promise of the Lord is that we will reign with Him; that is we will share in His royal authority.

Getting to heaven is what this life is all about. Jesus asks, *"What profit is there for one to gain the whole world and forfeit his life?* (Matthew 16:26) He was speaking of the life of heaven! We cannot begin to imagine the life of heaven for as St. Paul said, *"What eye has not seen, and ear has not heard, and what has not entered the human heart, what God has prepared for those who love him."* It is so easy to get distracted by the things of this world, but we are not made for here, we are made for there.

2) Whose last instructions to the Apostles was to go out and teach all nations.

Let's take a look at the end of St. Matthew's gospel chapter 28:16-20:

> *The eleven disciples went to Galilee, to the mountain to which Jesus had ordered them. When they saw him, they worshiped, but they doubted. Then Jesus approached and said to them, "All power in heaven and on earth has been given to me. Go, therefore, and make disciples of all nations, baptizing them in the name of the Father, and of the Son, and of the Holy Spirit, teaching them to observe all that I have commanded you. And behold, I am with you always, until the end of the age."*

This passage is known as "the great commission." Many Catholics are not aware that the end of Mass is patterned on this. In fact, the word "Mass" comes for the Latin word for send. In the early church they referred to the celebration of the Holy Eucharist as "the breaking of the bread," but we call it "Mass" to emphasize that we are now sent out into the world to proclaim the saving message of Jesus.

There is a lot in this little passage which we will examine in this reflection and the next. First, we have the issue of authority. Jesus says how all authority has been given to Him, but now He is sending them out to carry on His saving work. He is sending them to teach. He had earlier pointed out that a teacher has authority over the students (Matthew 10:24). The Lord tells them that they are to teach others to observe all that He had taught them. He expresses no concern that they will distort the message. Why Is that? We will see in the next mystery (the Descent of the Holy Spirit) how He will promise that the Holy Spirit will lead them to all truth.

He is commissioning them to transform the world and promises that He will be with them until the end of time. While His Church will face trials and tribulations Jesus never expresses concern that they will lose or twist His original message because He was not leaving them orphaned; He would be with them. His Holy Spirit would guide them.

207

In future Mysteries we will see how Jesus will keep this promise to be with the leaders of His people to the end of time, but for now it is essential to know that Jesus has never abandoned His Church.

3) Whose last instructions to His Apostles was to baptize all nations in the name of the Father, the Son, and the Holy Spirit.

Notice Jesus does not say to baptize "the adult of all nations." He says nothing about baptizing those old enough to accept Him as Lord and Savior. No, He tells them to baptize all nations. That would imply all people.

In the first Luminous Mystery we pointed out how Jesus tells us that we cannot be saved "unless you are born of water and Spirit." We showed how on the day of His baptism He transformed baptism from a mere ceremony to a means of receiving His saving grace. There are some however, who see baptism only as a ceremony that should take place only after the person has received Jesus as their personal Lord and Savior (a phrase found nowhere in the Bible). But we see here that the last words out of His mouth before the Ascension was to baptize all nations.

Historically we see the earliest Christians baptizing people of all ages. In the NT it never says that they baptized infants or toddlers, but we are told several times that entire households were baptized (see Acts 2:38-39, 11:14, 16:15 &31 &33, also 1 Cor 1:16). Certainly there is nowhere in the NT that tells us not to baptize children. In fact, Jesus Himself tells us that the Kingdom of Heaven belongs to the little ones in Luke 18:15-16:

> *"People were bringing even infants to him that he might touch them, and when the disciples saw this, they rebuked them.*

Jesus, however, called the children to himself and said, "Let the children come to me and do not prevent them; for the kingdom of God belongs to such as these.

If the Kingdom of God belongs to infants and baptism is the way into the Kingdom, why would any follower of Christ not bring their little ones to Him?

In the OT we see that the way to enter into the covenant with God was through circumcision and that was done on babies who were eight days old. If in the Old Covenant infants were to be brought in to the household of faith it would make no sense to fail to have infants come into the household of faith in the New. To not bring infants into the faith would be a departure from what was then biblical norms and certainly would warrant an explicit command to not baptize infants if that was the Will of God.

People bringing their children to receive God's saving grace through water and Spirit seems very much in keeping in with the prophecy of Isaiah where we are told in Is 44:3, *"I will pour out water upon the thirsty ground, streams upon the dry land; I will pour out my spirit upon your offspring, my blessing upon your descendants."* As human being we come into this world as thirsty ground yearning for the Lord who alone can satisfy the deepest longings in our hearts. In the waters of baptism God shares His very life with us. A parent can give his/her child no greater gift than God's saving grace in baptism.

Finally, historically we see that the debate occurring in the first two centuries of the Church was whether or not a family had to wait until the 8th day to have their children baptized. The answer was that there was no need to wait, a baby could be baptized immediately. The truth is that the issue of infant baptism did not come up for over 1500 years into Christianity. If we look to the entire Bible and to ancient Tradition, it is very clear that infants should be baptized.

4) Who took His place at the right hand of the Father.

5) Who took His place as the Lord of lords and King of kings.

> *So then the Lord Jesus, after he spoke to them, was taken up into heaven and took his seat at the right hand of God. (Mark 16:19)*

> *They said, "If you are the Messiah, tell us," but he replied to them, "If I tell you, you will not believe, and if I question, you will not respond. But from this time on the Son of Man will be seated at the right hand of the power of God." (Luke 22:67-69)*

> *Exalted at the right hand of God, he received the promise of the Holy Spirit from the Father and poured it forth, as you (both) see and hear (Act 2:33)*

> *I charge [you] before God, who gives life to all things, and before Christ Jesus, who gave testimony under Pontius Pilate for the noble confession to keep the commandment without stain or reproach until the appearance of our Lord Jesus Christ that the blessed and only ruler will make manifest at the proper time, the King of kings and Lord of lords, who alone has immortality, who dwells in unapproachable light, and whom no human being has seen or can see. To him be honor and eternal power. Amen. (1 Timothy 6:15)*

They will fight with the Lamb, but the Lamb will conquer them, for he is Lord of lords and king of kings, and those with him are called, chosen, and faithful." (Rev 17:14)

He has a name written on his cloak and on his thigh, "King of kings and Lord of lords." (Rev 19:16)

As we strive to live and proclaim our faith it is easy at times to be discouraged. We are tempted to despair of our own weaknesses; we become frustrated with the state of the world and the foolishness of the political elite. Sometimes we can feel the world is definitely going in the wrong direction and can believe that all is lost. At those times we need to remember that Jesus is the Lord of lords and King of kings! He has already won the victory! He is on the throne! No matter how bad things seem to get all we need to do is strive to remain faithful (we all falter to one degree or another) and we will share in His victory! He is the Lord of lords and King of kings and we can trust that He will make all things work out right in the end for those who love Him (Rom 8:28)!

6) God in the flesh who was adored by the angels.

Here we get into a little speculative theology. The Bible is clear that the angels now worship Jesus as God as we see in the following verses of scripture:

And again, when he leads the first-born into the world, he says: "Let all the angels of God worship him." (Heb 1:6)

...through the resurrection of Jesus Christ, who has gone into heaven and is at the right hand of God, with angels, authorities, and powers subject to him. (1 Peter 3:21b-22)

211

*I looked again and heard the voices of many angels who surrounded the throne and the living creatures and the elders. They were countless **in number**, and they cried out in a loud voice: "Worthy is the Lamb that was slain to receive power and riches, wisdom and strength, honor and glory and blessing."*

Then I heard every creature in heaven and on earth and under the earth and in the sea, everything in the universe, cry out: "To the one who sits on the throne and to the Lamb be blessing and honor, glory and might, forever and ever." The four living creatures answered, "Amen," and the elders fell down and worshiped.

It is traditionally believed that one of the things that led to the fall of the angels was that God gave them a foreknowledge that He would become a human being and that the angels would worship Him in the flesh and they would serve people. The idea that they would have to serve human being was unbearable to Satan and his followers. The idea that they would worship God in the form of a creature inferior to themselves was unthinkable to Satan and other fallen angels. Christ is worshipped by the angels in His Body. Satan and his followers rebelled at what they saw as God's ridiculous plans. This is one of the reasons that Satan and his demons hate us so much, we are the reason they fell from God's grace.

But it goes even beyond that. Human beings have an intimacy with God that the angels were never given. Right now, all who have been baptized are a part of "the Body of Christ." Christ sits at the right hand of the father in His Body. Which means you and I sit at the right hand of the Father right now. And the angels worship God in the flesh.

The faithful angels embraced God Will and His plans. Embracing God's Will took incredible humility on their part. They now worship God in the flesh and willingly give of themselves to help creatures who by nature are very much inferior to themselves. That was God's plan and the faithful angels with joy embrace and humbly carry out that plan. They love God, His holy Will and us; the demons on the other hand reject God, His holy Will and hate us.

7) Who trusted Peter who denied Him to be the leader of His Church.

As one reads through the NT it is clear that Peter had a special place in God's plan of salvation. We have already seen how Jesus prayed that Peter's faith would never fail (Lk 22: 31-32); that He changed his name from Simon to Peter and entrusted him with the keys of the kingdom (Mt 16:13-19); and how Jesus the Good Shepherd entrusted the shepherds staff to Peter (Jn 21:15-19). We also see that Peter is mentioned by name 195 times, more often in the NT than any other Apostle (coming in at #2 is John at 29 mentions); When all 12 names are mentioned Peter is always mentioned first; on a number of occasions the Apostles are referred to as, "Peter and his companions (Lk 9:32) or Peter and the rest of the Apostles (Mk 16:7 & Acts 2:37). It is Peter who decides that there should be a replacement for Judas and organizes the process of selecting a replacement (Acts 1:15-26). At the Council of Jerusalem when there is great debate about the issue of circumcision and whether it was necessary for Gentiles coming into the Church to keep all the OT ritual laws, we are told that Peter spoke and the debate ended (Acts 15:1-12). By any reasonable and objective standard, it is clear that Peter was the leader of the Apostles and had a special place in the early Church.

But Peter is often most remembered for denying that he even knew Jesus. And yet that is the man who the Lord called to be the leader of His Church after He ascended into heaven. Even though Peter was far from perfect he was chosen by the Lord to be the leader of His Kingdom on earth. Peter's sinfulness and denial did not make Him ineligible for that important role.

8) Who trusted the Apostles who abandoned Him to carry on His saving work.

If the failures of God's chosen ones made them ineligible for the exalted role God calls them too, then the Apostles would have needed to be replaced, but they were not. Despite their failure of courage; even though after He was arrested the Apostles fled; despite the fact that the Apostles (with the exception of St. John) were nowhere to be found as Jesus was crucified; Jesus still trusted them with the important task of carrying on His saving work!

We have already seen how when Jesus appeared to the Apostles after the Resurrection, He did not scold or chastise them. Instead He gave them the power to forgive sins (Jn 20:19-23). Earlier He had said to the disciples, *"Whoever listens to you listens to me. Whoever rejects you rejects me. And whoever rejects me rejects the one who sent me."* (Lk 10:16)

The amazing truth is that the Lord entrusted incredible authority, His own authority to the Apostles, and their failures did not nullify that authority.

We often hear people justify their leaving the Catholic Church to "the bad popes" and the "corrupt clergy" over the centuries or "the abuses of the Church", but that is not the criteria that Jesus uses. His ministers

214

do not have to be perfect; His ministers can and often do fail in the pursuit of holiness and perfection, but that does not nullify their authority. We see Jesus teach this very truth in Mt 23:1-3a,

> *Then Jesus spoke to the crowds and to his disciples, saying, "The scribes and the Pharisees have taken their seat on the chair of Moses. Therefore, do and observe all things whatsoever they tell you, but do not follow their example."*

He will go on to call them hypocrites, blind guides and fools, but He starts out by commanding the people to obey them because they have the authority entrusted to Moses! Jesus tells a parable of a man who has authority entrusted to him by the master; and the man abuses that authority and Jesus does not say the man forfeits his authority, but rather that the master will deal with the man (Mt 24:45-51).

Throughout the OT we see many of the patriarchs, clergy and kings fall short of what God calls them too, and yet God never tells the people that the man who fell short forfeits his authority. There are times when God Himself will remove someone from office (Shebna in Isaiah 22 for instance), the Lord never tells those under the person's authority that they no longer have to obey. Certainly, the greatest example of this is Israel's first king, Saul. He had lost the favor of God and the Lord had determined that his son would not succeed him to the throne. God chose David to be the next king and had the prophet anoint him to be the next king. We see King Saul attempting to kill David. David had the opportunity to kill Saul on two occasions and refuses to do so because Saul, as sinful as he was, continued to be God's anointed (see 1 Samuel 24:1-8 and 1 Samuel 26:1-11).

215

The Bible is clear, God's chosen are not perfect; they often fail to live up to the role God has entrusted to them, but their sinfulness does not nullify their God given authority!

9) Who trusts me, though a sinner, to be His instrument in the world today.

The dignity that our good and gracious God bestows upon each of us is incredible. He has made us His children and co-workers with Christ in the on-going work of salvation. He bestows this dignity upon us even though we are far from perfect. He of course wants us to strive for perfection for as He teaches in Mt 5:48, *"So be perfect, just as your heavenly Father is perfect."* And yet despite the imperfection that persists in our lives He elevates us to be His sons and daughters and allows us to be instruments for people's salvation in the world. The greatness of His love and the dignity He bestows on His people is beyond words!

10) Who ascended into heaven to prepare a place for His faithful people. (P)

We end where we began with the idea that our true home is in heaven. He wants us to share eternal life with Him, but He will not force Himself on any of us. God gives us freedom! We can choose for Him or against. God showers His grace on us so that we will choose for Him, but He continues to allow us freedom. We can resist His grace if we choose. We can refuse to see His handiwork in the world. We can deny His existence or refuse His Lordship over our lives. He has prepared a place for His faithful people, if we choose to strive for fidelity we will be with Him forever; if we choose to turn our backs to Him He will respect our choice. Let us choose to be His faithful people

*Holy Mary, Mother of God, pray for us sinners
now and at the hour of our death. Amen.*

*Glory be to the Father,
and to the Son, and to the Holy Spirit:
As it was in the beginning,
is now, and ever shall be, world without end. Amen*

*Oh my Jesus, forgive our sins and save us from the power of hell.
Lead all souls into heaven especially those
most in need of your mercy. Amen*

The Third Glorious Mystery
The Descent of the Holy Spirit

*Hail Mary, full of grace, the Lord is with you; blessed are you among women, and blessed is the fruit of your womb, **Jesus**:*

1) Who promised to send His Holy Spirit to guide us in all truth. (P)

Let's take a look at the promises that Jesus Himself made:

> *And I will ask the Father, and he will give you another Advocate to be with you always, the Spirit of truth, which the world cannot accept, because it neither sees nor knows it. But you know it, because it remains with you, and will be in you. I will not leave you orphans...* (Jn 14:16-18a)

> *"I have much more to tell you, but you cannot bear it now. But when he comes, the Spirit of truth, he will guide you to all truth. He will not speak on his own, but he will speak what he hears, and will declare to you the things that are coming. He will glorify me, because he will take from what is mine and declare it to you.* (Jn16:12-14}

Do you believe that Jesus kept His promise? Many Christians do not believe. After all Jesus did not say, "I will send the Spirit, so you can know some of the truth"; or "You can know some of the truth mixed with error"; and He certainly did not say, "There will be no divinely revealed truth, everyone must decide for themselves what they want to believe." No, Jesus said He would send the Holy Spirit so that we could know the truth. And yet, many believe we cannot know the

218

truth, so everyone must decide for themselves what is true for them. Do you believe Jesus kept His promise?

It is important to recognize that the above promises of Jesus were made only to the Apostles as He shared the Last Supper with them. This was not a promise made to the crowds or even to all disciples, it was made to the Apostles.

If Jesus did keep His promise, there must be somewhere I can personally turn to in order to be assured of knowing the truth. Where is the fullness of truth? According to the Bible the source you and I can turn to is the Church. That is what St. Paul tells us in 1 Timothy 3:15, *"But if I should be delayed, you should know how to behave in the household of God, which is the church of the living God, the pillar and foundation of truth."* The promise Jesus made was not to individual Christians, but to the Church as a whole. It was made to the shepherds of the Church.

We see how this is to play out throughout history when we study the first major crisis that the Church faced. In the Bible itself we see how there were Christians who argued that gentiles coming into the Church needed to follow the entire Mosaic Law, including circumcision. That of course would have been a huge obstacle to people coming into the Church! A decision had to be made. As we look at the scriptures on this issue we do not see the Apostles say to people, "You have to decide for yourselves what God wants you to do." We do not see them say, "Pray about it and the Holy Spirit will lead you personally to decide what is right for you." No, it is the leaders of the Church who had the sure knowledge that the Holy Spirit would guide them who decisively settled the matter. Let's take a look at this as it appears in Acts 15: 1- 29:

Some who had come down from Judea were instructing the brothers, "Unless you are circumcised according to the Mosaic practice, you cannot be saved." Because there arose no little dissension and debate by Paul and Barnabas with them, it was decided that Paul, Barnabas, and some of the others should go up to Jerusalem to the apostles and presbyters about this question. They were sent on their journey by the church, and passed through Phoenicia and Samaria telling of the conversion of the Gentiles, and brought great joy to all the brothers. When they arrived in Jerusalem, they were welcomed by the Church, as well as by the apostles and the presbyters, and they reported what God had done with them. But some from the party of the Pharisees who had become believers stood up and said, "It is necessary to circumcise them and direct them to observe the Mosaic law."

The apostles and the presbyters met together to see about this matter.

After much debate had taken place, Peter got up and said to them, "My brothers, you are well aware that from early days God made his choice among you that through my mouth the Gentiles would hear the word of the gospel and believe. And God, who knows the heart, bore witness by granting them the Holy Spirit just as he did us. He made no distinction between us and them, for by faith he purified their hearts. Why, then, are you now putting God to the test by placing on the shoulders of the disciples a yoke that neither our ancestors nor we have been able to bear? On the contrary, we believe that we are saved through the grace of the Lord Jesus, in the same way as they." The whole assembly fell silent, and they listened while

Paul and Barnabas described the signs and wonders God had worked among the Gentiles through them.

After they had fallen silent, James responded, "My brothers, listen to me. Simeon has described how God first concerned himself with acquiring from among the Gentiles a people for his name. The words of the prophets agree with this, as is written:

'After this I shall return and rebuild the fallen hut of David; from its ruins I shall rebuild it and raise it up again, so that the rest of humanity may seek out the Lord, even all the Gentiles on whom my name is invoked. Thus says the Lord who accomplishes these things, known from of old.' It is my judgment, therefore, that we ought to stop troubling the Gentiles who turn to God, but tell them by letter to avoid pollution from idols, unlawful marriage, the meat of strangled animals, and blood. For Moses, for generations now, has had those who proclaim him in every town, as he has been read in the synagogues every Sabbath." Then the apostles and presbyters, in agreement with the whole church, decided to choose representatives and to send them to Antioch with Paul and Barnabas. The ones chosen were Judas, who was called Barsabbas, and Silas, leaders among the brothers. This is the letter delivered by them: "The apostles and the presbyters, your brothers, to the brothers in Antioch, Syria, and Cilicia of Gentile origin: greetings. Since we have heard that some of our number [who went out] without any mandate from us have upset you with their teachings and disturbed your peace of mind, we have with one accord decided to choose representatives and to send them to you along with our beloved Barnabas and Paul, who have dedicated their lives to the name

221

of our Lord Jesus Christ. So we are sending Judas and Silas who will also convey this same message by word of mouth: 'It is the decision of the Holy Spirit and of us not to place on you any burden beyond these necessities, namely, to abstain from meat sacrificed to idols, from blood, from meats of strangled animals, and from unlawful marriage. If you keep free of these, you will be doing what is right. Farewell.'"

In this passage you will notice that in verses 11 &12 that Peter speaks and the whole assembly becomes quiet. Peter had spoken the matter was settled. In vs 24 we were told that the people who were causing problems had not been authorized by the Apostles to teach what they were teaching. The clear implication was that it was necessary to be authorized by the Apostles to teach the faith. But most importantly we see in vs 28 that this decision was not a matter of personal opinion, it was the decision of the Holy Spirit! The biblical model is when issues arise, the leaders of the Church are to gather with Peter (or his successor) and the decision would have the sure guidance of the Holy Spirit.

This is how important decisions have always been settled in the history of the Church. Over the centuries there were many opinions as to who Jesus is. Some said He was God; others argued He was just a man; others said He was a man adopted by God to become His son. Which was it? Is Jesus the eternal Son of God or merely a creature? Knowing who Jesus is would be essential to having a relationship with Him. It was declared that Jesus is the eternal Son of God.

There were debates about who God was. All Christians today recognize the Trinity, but that is a word that is not found in the Bible, and there was great debate about it in the first centuries of the Church. But we have the biblical model as to how the followers of Jesus could know the truth. It was not by personally praying about it and deciding for oneself. It was by the leaders of the Church gathering together with the successor of Peter (or his representatives) and making a decision as to what the Holy Spirit had revealed. Christian doctrine is not opinion, it is the revelation of God Himself.

The questions every individual Christian must ask him/herself are these: "Do I believe that Jesus kept His promise to guide us in all truth? Do I believe the Bible when it teaches that the Church is the pillar and foundation of all truth? As I stated earlier, most Christians today do not believe Jesus kept His promise. Most do not believe that the Church is the pillar and foundation of all truth. But that certainly raises the question of what faith consists of. After all, if I do not believe Jesus kept His promise can I really claim to "believe in Jesus"? If I do not believe that the Church is the pillar and foundation of all truth can I really claim to believe the Bible is God's inerrant Word since the Bible does teach that?

As Catholics we believe it is essential to faith to affirm that Jesus kept His promise. Do you believe that Jesus kept His promise? Your salvation might depend on it!

2) Whose Apostles prayed for nine days for the coming of the Spirit.

This points us to a little Catholic trivia. This is the beginning of Catholics praying novenas. A novena is a nine day, nine week, or nine month prayer. The key is the number nine. The Apostles prayed for nine days for the outpouring of the Spirit when their prayers were answered. As Catholics we often follow their example in praying a novena.

3) Whose Apostles were praying with Mary when the Holy Spirit came upon them.

It would appear that Mary is a real Holy Spirit magnet. We saw how she was the first person in the NT that the Holy Spirit would descend upon (Mt 1:20, Lk 1:35); when Mary went to the home of her kinswoman the Holy Spirit filled Elizabeth (Lk 1:41-42); and in the Acts of the Apostles we are told that when the Apostles returned to Jerusalem after the Ascension that they were praying with Mary and some others (Act 1:14). We are then told after the choice of Matthias to be the successor of Judas how "...they were all in one place together." Christian tradition has always placed Mary with the Apostles at this holy moment.

Even today in the charismatic movement in the Church there is great devotion to the Blessed Mother. Mary really is a Holy Spirit magnate, as we grow closer to her the more the Holy Spirit will be a part of our lives.

4) Who sent the Holy Spirit in the form of a mighty wind.

As we discuss the outpouring of the Holy Spirit it would be helpful to look at Acts2: 1- 41:

> When the time for Pentecost was fulfilled, they were all in one place together. And suddenly there came from the sky a noise like a strong driving wind, and it filled the entire house in which they were. Then there appeared to them tongues as of fire, which parted and came to rest on each one of them. And they were all filled with the Holy Spirit and began to speak in different tongues, as the Spirit enabled them to proclaim.

224

Now there were devout Jews from every nation under heaven staying in Jerusalem. At this sound, they gathered in a large crowd, but they were confused because each one heard them speaking in his own language. They were astounded, and in amazement they asked, "Are not all these people who are speaking Galileans? Then how does each of us hear them in his own native language? We are Parthians, Medes, and Elamites, inhabitants of Mesopotamia, Judea and Cappadocia, Pontus and Asia, Phrygia and Pamphylia, Egypt and the districts of Libya near Cyrene, as well as travelers from Rome, both Jews and converts to Judaism, Cretans and Arabs, yet we hear them speaking in our own tongues of the mighty acts of God." They were all astounded and bewildered, and said to one another, "What does this mean?" But others said, scoffing, "They have had too much new wine."

Then Peter stood up with the Eleven, raised his voice, and proclaimed to them, "You who are Jews, indeed all of you staying in Jerusalem. Let this be known to you, and listen to my words. These people are not drunk, as you suppose, for it is only nine o'clock in the morning. No, this is what was spoken through the prophet Joel: 'It will come to pass in the last days,' God says, 'that I will pour out a portion of my spirit upon all flesh.

Your sons and your daughters shall prophesy, your young men shall see visions, your old men shall dream dreams. Indeed, upon my servants and my handmaids I will pour out a portion of my spirit in those days, and they shall prophesy. And I will work wonders in the heavens above and signs on the earth below: blood, fire, and a cloud of smoke. The sun shall be turned to darkness, and the moon to blood, before the coming of the great and splendid day of the Lord, and it shall be that everyone shall be saved who calls on the name of the Lord.' You who are Israelites, hear these words. Jesus the Nazorean was a man commended to you by God with mighty deeds, wonders, and signs, which God worked through him in your midst, as you yourselves know. This man, delivered up by the set plan and foreknowledge of God, you killed, using lawless men to crucify him. But God raised him up, releasing him from the throes of death, because it was impossible for him to be held by it. For David says of him: 'I saw the Lord ever before me, with him at my right hand I shall not be disturbed. Therefore, my heart has been glad and my tongue has exulted; my flesh, too, will dwell in hope, because you will not abandon my soul to the netherworld, nor will you suffer your holy one to see corruption. You have made known to me the paths of life; you will fill me with joy in your presence.'

My brothers, one can confidently say to you about the patriarch David that he died and was buried, and his tomb is in our midst to this day. But since he was a prophet and knew that God had sworn an oath to him that he would set one of his descendants upon his throne, he foresaw and spoke of the resurrection of the Messiah, that neither was he abandoned to the netherworld nor did his flesh see corruption. God raised this Jesus; of this we are all witnesses. Exalted at the right hand of God, he received the promise of the Holy Spirit from the Father and poured it forth, as you (both) see and hear. For David did not go up into heaven, but he himself said: 'The Lord said to my Lord, "Sit at my right hand until I make your enemies your footstool."' Therefore let the whole house of Israel know for certain that God has made him both Lord and Messiah, this Jesus whom you crucified."

226

Now when they heard this, they were cut to the heart, and they asked Peter and the other apostles, "What are we to do, my brothers?" Peter [said] to them, "Repent and be baptized, every one of you, in the name of Jesus Christ for the forgiveness of your sins; and you will receive the gift of the Holy Spirit. For the promise is made to you and to your children and to all those far off, whomever the Lord our God will call." He testified with many other arguments, and was exhorting them, "Save yourselves from this corrupt generation." Those who accepted his message were baptized, and about three thousand persons were added that day.

It certainly would be helpful to notice several things we have already examined: that is Peter spoke on behalf of all the Apostles; that it was prophesized by David that the Savior would sit at the right hand of the Father; and that those who were being saved were all baptized.

But what we want to focus on here was that the Holy Spirit came in the form of a mighty wind. This helps us understand how Pentecost was the fulfilment of a type. In the introduction we spoke a little about typology. We pointed out how the fulfillment of a type is always far greater than the original type. We also saw that when we see something in the NT that resembles the original type we need to recognize how that helps us interpret correctly the original OT event.

In the first two verses of the Bible we are told, *"In the beginning, when God created the heavens and the earth — and the earth was without form or shape, with darkness over the abyss and a mighty wind sweeping over the waters"* (Gen 1:1-2). Reading back now into Genesis we see that the "mighty wind" was in fact the Holy Spirit. All of creation came from the waters and the Holy Spirit. This also gives us insight into baptism. All of creation came from "water and the Holy

Spirit" so when we are baptized we come out of the waters as a "new creation."

But if we follow the biblical principle that the fulfillment of a type is always greater than the original type we need to conclude that both Pentecost and baptism are greater events than the act of creation! How can that be? Well creation only had to do with the physical universe, while Pentecost and baptism both impart the life of God into the lives of individuals. God is greater than all of creation. So Pentecost and baptism are both greater events than when God created the universe. That is an incredible mystery that we do well to ponder!

5) Who sent the Holy Spirit in the form of tongues of fire. (P)

Why is it important to our salvation to know that the Holy Spirit came in the form of fire? It is once again to help us understand where the Holy Spirit was active throughout the OT. In the OT we see several different times when the "pillar of fire" is mentioned along with the "pillar of cloud" (Exodus 13:21&22,14:24, Numbers 14:14, Nehemiah 9:12&19). Fire and cloud are both signs of the Holy Spirit. Let's take a look at how the Israelites were saved as they passed through the waters of the Red Sea guided by the pillar of fire and pillar of cloud as it appears in Exodus 14:19-31:

> The angel of God, who had been leading Israel's army, now moved and went around behind them. And the column of cloud, moving from in front of them, took up its place behind them, so that it came between the Egyptian army and that of Israel. And when it became dark, the cloud illumined the night; and so the rival camps did not come any closer together all night long. Then Moses stretched out his hand over the sea; and the LORD drove back the sea with a strong east wind all night long and

turned the sea into dry ground. The waters were split, so that the Israelites entered into the midst of the sea on dry land, with the water as a wall to their right and to their left. The Egyptians followed in pursuit after them—all Pharaoh's horses and chariots and horsemen—into the midst of the sea. But during the watch just before dawn, the LORD looked down from a column of fiery cloud upon the Egyptian army and threw it into a panic; and he so clogged their chariot wheels that they could drive only with difficulty. With that the Egyptians said, "Let us flee from Israel, because the LORD is fighting for them against Egypt."

Then the LORD spoke to Moses: Stretch out your hand over the sea, that the water may flow back upon the Egyptians, upon their chariots and their horsemen. So Moses stretched out his hand over the sea, and at daybreak the sea returned to its normal flow. The Egyptians were fleeing head on toward it when the LORD cast the Egyptians into the midst of the sea. As the water flowed back, it covered the chariots and the horsemen. Of all Pharaoh's army which had followed the Israelites into the sea, not even one escaped. But the Israelites had walked on dry land through the midst of the sea, with the water as a wall to their right and to their left. Thus the LORD saved Israel on that day from the power of Egypt. When Israel saw the Egyptians lying dead on the seashore and saw the great power that the LORD had shown against Egypt, the people feared the LORD. They believed in the LORD and in Moses his servant.

As we read through the entire book of Exodus we see that the Holy Spirit appeared in the form of a "pillar of cloud" by day and a "pillar of fire" by night. So, on the day of Pentecost the "tongues of fire" was meant to recall to the Apostles how God had saved their ancestors through water and the sea. We see St. Paul explain that idea in 1 Cor 10: 1-13:

> *I do not want you to be unaware, brothers, that our ancestors were all under the cloud and all passed through the sea, and all of them were baptized into Moses in the cloud and in the sea. All ate the same spiritual food, and all drank the same spiritual drink, for they drank from a spiritual rock that followed them, and the rock was the Christ. Yet God was not pleased with most of them, for they were struck down in the desert.*
>
> *These things happened as examples for us, so that we might not desire evil things, as they did. And do not become idolaters, as some of them did, as it is written, "The people sat down to eat and drink, and rose up to revel." Let us not indulge in immorality as some of them did, and twenty-three thousand fell within a single day. Let us not test Christ as some of them did, and suffered death by serpents. Do not grumble as some of them did and suffered death by the destroyer. These things happened to them as an example, and they have been written down as a warning to us, upon whom the end of the ages has come. Therefore, whoever thinks he is standing secure should take care not to fall. No trial has come to you but what is human. God is faithful and will not let you be tried beyond your strength; but with the trial he will also provide a way out, so that you may be able to bear it.*

We see how important it is to read the Bible as a whole. It is also important to read the Bible in context. From the story of Pentecost, we go back to Exodus and we see how both fire and cloud are symbols of

230

the Holy Spirit. Reading the story of Exodus in light of Pentecost we see how in passing through the Red Sea it was the Holy Spirit leading the Israelites from slavery to a new life of freedom. St. Paul in I Corinthians then sees how the passing through the Red Sea was meant to be an image of baptism (an OT type) and actually says how OT Israel was "baptized into Moses."

6) Whose Holy Spirit filled the Apostles with courage and other gifts.

Jesus had promised to send the Holy Spirit upon the Apostles to lead them in all truth. He had promised that the Spirit would be a comforter, healer and consoler. He would not leave them as orphans.

In Catholic theology we speak of the seven gifts of the Holy Spirit, here I highlight one of them (although we can gain great spiritual insights by meditating on any of the gifts). The seven gifts are wisdom, understanding, counsel, courage, knowledge, piety (godliness,) and fear of the Lord. In addition, we have the fruits of the Spirit which are love, joy, peace, patience, kindness, generosity, faithfulness, gentleness, and self-control.

I highlight courage (although you are certainly free to focus on any of these gifts or fruits) because it is a gift that I feel I am most lacking (that is not to say that I have any of the gifts in abundance). In our day and age, it takes courage to give witness to Jesus at work, at family gatherings, in our neighborhoods. We fear being labeled as fanatics, or cult like, or extremists. As a result, we are surrounded by people who desperately need to come to know Jesus, but they rarely hear about Him from us. The second command of faith of course is to love our neighbor as ourselves and yet there are people around us who do not have the gift of faith (a necessary gift for salvation) and we are often reluctant to share the faith with them. What kind of love is that? People could be on their way to an eternity away from God and we are uneasy about sharing the gospel that can save them because we do not want them to be uncomfortable. As followers of Christ we need to have the courage to be impolite enough to lead people to salvation.

7) Whose Apostles won 3,000 converts on the day of Pentecost.

The Apostles during the earthly ministry of Jesus certainly did not appear to be capable of leading vast amounts of people to the Lord. And yet by the power of the Holy Spirit we see them do great things! This gives me great hope! Like the Apostles by nature I am not the sharpest knife in the draw, but by the power of the Holy Spirit even I can accomplish great things. By the power of the Holy Spirit you can do great things as well!

8) Who sends the Holy Spirit to change bread and wine into His holy Body and Precious Blood.

9) Who sends the Holy Spirit so that all the sacraments will be efficacious.

The Holy Spirit was poured out upon the Apostles on the day of Pentecost, but that was not the end! The Holy Spirit continues to work in and through the Church. When the Church does what Jesus commands us to do in celebrating the sacraments the Holy Spirit continues to bestow grace. God works through His Church to bestow His saving grace. Let's take a look at a few passages that makes this abundantly clear:

> *In it he also went to preach to the spirits in prison, who had once been disobedient while God patiently waited in the days*

of Noah during the building of the ark, in which a few persons, eight in all, were saved through water. This prefigured baptism, which saves you now (1 Peter 3:19-21a)

For I received from the Lord what I also handed on to you, that the Lord Jesus, on the night he was handed over, took bread, and, after he had given thanks, broke it and said, "This is my body that is for you. Do this in remembrance of me." In the same way also the cup, after supper, saying, "This cup is the new covenant in my blood. Do this, as often as you drink it, in remembrance of me.' For as often as you eat this bread and drink the cup, you proclaim the death of the Lord until he comes.

Therefore, whoever eats the bread or drinks the cup of the Lord unworthily will have to answer for the body and blood of the Lord. A person should examine himself, and so eat the bread and drink the cup. For anyone who eats and drinks without discerning the body, eats and drinks judgment on himself. (1 Cor 11:23-29).

He said in reply, "Have you not read that from the beginning the Creator 'made them male and female' and said, 'For this reason a man shall leave his father and mother and be joined to his wife, and the two shall become one flesh'? So they are no longer two, but one flesh. Therefore, what God has joined together, no human being must separate." (Mt 19:4-6)

Is anyone among you sick? He should summon the presbyters of the church, and they should pray over him and anoint [him] with oil in the name of the Lord, and the prayer of faith will

233

save the sick person, and the Lord will raise him up. If he has committed any sins, he will be forgiven (James 5:14-15).

[Jesus] said to them again, "Peace be with you. As the Father has sent me, so I send you." And when he had said this, he breathed on them and said to them, "Receive the Holy Spirit. Whose sins you forgive are forgiven them, and whose sins you retain are retained" (John 20:21-23).

All the above passages speak of the celebration of various sacraments. In the first one from 1 Peter it speaks of how baptism saves people. It does not say anything about, "unless the minister of baptism was unworthy" or "unless the person was unworthy at the time he or she received baptism;" no, it presumes when an individual is baptized that the person does receive grace.

In the second passage from 1 Corinthians it presumes that the bread and wine becomes the Body and Blood of the Lord. There are again no ifs, ands, or buts about it; at Mass the bread and wine becomes the Body and Blood of Christ and it is essential that a person only come forward to receive when they believe in the real presence and are in a state of grace (see verses 27-29).

In the third passage from Matthew 19 about marriage Jesus makes it clear that when the Church performs a wedding that it is actually God who marries the couple. I have been to many weddings, but have never seen God in all His glory come and pronounce the man and woman husband and wife. That is done by an official representative of the Church and state (in some cases just the state), and yet Jesus says that it is God Himself who unites them to become one.

The fourth passage we have already examined, but notice Jesus does not say, "Some of the time you forgive sins they will be forgiven and sometimes they will not be." No, whenever the official representative of the Church forgives sins they will be forgiven them.

Finally, the fifth passage from James about the anointing of the sick. James speaks in absolute terms. Whenever the "presbyter" (which is where we get the word priest) anoints the person God's grace will be given. The person anointed will receive God's forgiveness and will find healing (spiritual, emotional and sometimes physical). Again, there are no ifs, ands or buts presented by the inspired author. The bottom line is that the sacraments are efficacious (meaning that they always convey God's grace when they are validly celebrated). They are always efficacious because the power of the Holy Spirit continues to work in and through the Church that Jesus established.

10) Who promised to send the Holy Spirit so that we can know the truth. (P)

We end where we began, with the promise of Jesus. We can know about God and how He works in the world because Jesus kept His promise to send the Holy Spirit to guide His Church in all truth. As Catholics we can look at the history of the Church with all the scandals, intrigues, and obvious failures of various popes, cardinals, bishops, priests, deacons, nuns, and lay people and we can proclaim, "God is so great! Look how He has faithfully preserved the truth even through these clowns!" After all He preserved the truth through the Apostles and the writers of scripture and they were not always the bravest, holiest or most faithful people on the face of the earth. Why would anyone doubt that the God who preserved the truth through the Apostles would somehow be incapable of preserving the truth through the Borgia popes, corrupt bishops, or scandalous priests or nuns? We can be assured that the teaching of the Church is true not because of the holiness of those who hold high office in the Church, but because Jesus Christ is always true to His Word! You can bet your salvation on that fact! You can also put your salvation at great risk by denying that Jesus kept His promise.

Holy Mary, Mother of God, pray for us sinners
now and at the hour of our death. Amen.

Glory be to the Father,
and to the Son, and to the Holy Spirit:
As it was in the beginning,
is now, and ever shall be, world without end. Amen

Oh my Jesus, forgive our sins and save us from the power of hell.
Lead all souls into heaven especially those
most in need of your mercy. Amen

The Fourth Glorious Mystery
The Assumption of Mary

*Hail Mary, full of grace, the Lord is with you; blessed are you among women, and blessed is the fruit of your womb, **Jesus:***

1) Who like all the kings in the line of David brought His Mother into His throne room. (P)

When we go through the OT books of Kings it is clear that the mother of the King in the Kingdom of Judah had an exalted role. As you go through the books they speak of the new king, the age he was when he ascended to the throne and who his mother was. There are a few exceptions, most likely when the king's mother was deceased. For instance, we see in 1 Kings 15:10 when it tells us who the grandmother of King Asa was. But a few verses later it tells us how Asa removed his grandmother from the position of "queen mother" because of her sinfulness.

One of the interesting things about the books of Kings is that it almost never mentions who the mother of the king of Israel is (that is the northern kingdom that had pulled away from Judah and the Davidic kings), but it always tells the reader who the "Queen Mother" was in the kingdom of David's ancestors.

First century Jewish Christians who were steeped in the OT would certainly have expected the King in the line of David, to give a place of honor to His Mother. In fact, to not give honor to His Mother would have been a huge departure from the biblical model and would certainly have required an explanation as to why the Davidic King would have made such a radical departure from biblical norms.

237

We will examine this phenomenon of the honor afforded to the mother of the king in the line of David more thoroughly in the next Mystery of the Coronation.

2) Who prepared a special place for His Mother.

In Revelation 12:14 we are told of how Satan is attacking "the woman" (Mary) and how she is taken to a special place where she is nourished. The basic teaching of the Catholic Church is that Jesus has prepared a special place for His mom in His Kingdom. We will examine the depths of that in the Mystery on the Coronation, but for now we need to ponder why some Christians are so adamantly opposed to the idea that Mary has a special place in Jesus' Kingdom. After all, the Bible is clear that Mary has a special role in salvation history.

3) Who brought His Mother body and soul to heaven at the end of her earthly life.

Most Christians, including most Catholics believe that Mary died. Although the Church has never officially declared that she left this world through death, most Catholic theologians believed that she did in fact die. In the Eastern Church they celebrate the Feast of "the Dormition (falling asleep) of Mary."

The question that comes from this is, "If death came into the world as a result of sin and Mary was never tainted by sin, why did she die? Most theologians argue that she died to conform her life more fully with the life of her Son. Jesus died and rose, to more fully conform her life to His she also shared in the reality of death.

But from earliest times it was believed that Mary was brought body and soul into the glory of heaven. In Revelation 12 (which we will examine in the next mystery) we see Mary appearing in heaven clothed with the sun, the moon under her feet and on her head a crown of 12 stars. In other words, she is described as having a body in heaven. In the early Church the Christians of various cities, towns and villages used to brag about which holy person's bodily remains they had on hand. Having the relics of a holy martyr or hero of the faith gave them bragging rights. And yet we never see any city, town or village claim to have the bodily remains of the Blessed Mother, why? Because right from the beginning it was believed that Mary was taken body and soul to heaven. Although the "Assumption of Mary" was only officially declared a dogma of the faith in 1950 by Pope Pius XII, it was not a new belief. For centuries Catholics had prayed the Rosary and the Assumption of Mary was the 4th Glorious Mystery. Pope Pius XII officially declared this ancient belief dogma because he believed it would be spiritually beneficial for the Church and world to ponder this great mystery at the time.

4) Who prefigured Mary's Assumption in the life of Enoch.

In Genesis 5:24 we are told, *"Enoch walked with God, and he was no longer here, for God took him."* The author of Hebrews in chapter 11:5 interprets this for us when he states, *"By faith Enoch was taken up so that he should not see death, and "he was found no more because God had taken him." Before he was taken up, he was attested to have pleased God."* The idea of an assumption into heaven is not a strange concept in the Bible, in fact we will see that it is a promise of God to all His faithful people. We are eventually to be brought body and soul to heaven (see 1 Thessalonians 4:16-17).

The OT "assumptions" we will discuss were certainly not seen as the norm throughout the history of God's people. Throughout the OT it is presumed that the gates of heaven were closed and those who died went to a shadowy existence in "Sheol," which is often translated into English as "the netherworld," "the underworld," or even "Hades." 1 Peter 3:19 tells us how Jesus went to preach to the souls of those "in prison." This captures the OT idea that people who died did not go to heaven because the gates were closed. But as we will see, there were three exceptions to this belief, the first of whom was Enoch.

5) Who prefigured Mary's Assumption in the life of Elijah.

In 2 Kings 2:1 & 11 we read, *"When the LORD was about to take Elijah up to heaven in a whirlwind, he and Elisha were on their way from Gilgal...As they walked on still conversing, a fiery chariot and fiery horses came between the two of them, and Elijah went up to heaven in a whirlwind..."*

So once again we see the idea of a person who was very faithful to the Lord being brought body and soul into heaven. There are many today who believe this belief of Catholics that Mary was brought body and soul into heaven is "unbiblical." And while the Bible does not explicitly describe Mary's Assumption as Elijah's was, the idea of an assumption into heaven is certainly very much a part of the teaching of the Bible, in other words it is not "unbiblical." Couple that with the fact that all kings in the line of David brought their mothers into their throne room and that "the woman" in Revelation 12 is described as being in heaven in bodily form, there is really no serious reason to question the Assumption of our Lady into heaven body and soul.

240

6) Who prefigured the Assumption of Mary in the life of Moses.

The assumption of Moses into heaven resembles the Assumption of Mary more than the other two. First, Moses died. As we already discussed most Catholic theologians believe that Mary also experienced death at the end of her earthly life. But secondly, the Bible, unlike in the case of Enoch and Elijah, does not explicitly say that Moses was brought body and soul to heaven. In Jude 1:9 we are told that the Archangel Michael contended with Satan over the body of Moses, but this idea is not found in the OT. There were some Jewish apocryphal works entitled "The Assumption of Moses" and "the Testament of Moses" that have the idea of Moses being brought body and soul to heaven.

In the gospels in the story of the Transfiguration we see Moses and Elijah appear with Jesus. In those stories there is no indication that Moses appeared in a different form than Elijah. As we have already seen Elijah was taken body and soul to heaven, it would be odd for the gospel writers to not make some distinction if Moses appeared in ghostly form while Elijah appeared in bodily form.

7) Who made His Mother a sign of hope for all His faithful.

8) Who will's His faithful see His gifts to Mary as promises to themselves.

Throughout the Bible we see how God uses symbols to convey His Divine truth to the world. The whole principle of typology is that people, places and things in the OT were meant to prefigure or point us to people, places or things in the NT. In the gospel of John, he uses the phrase "the beloved disciple" or "the disciple who Jesus loved" in speaking of himself. But he did that so that he could be a representative of all Jesus' disciples.

In the OT we see how God commanded the Prophet Hosea to take a harlot for a wife. She and her children were to represent to Israel how God viewed the nation as an unfaithful spouse. So poor Hosea took Gomer as his bride which had to lead to a life of heartache and pain. Her children were named Lo-ruhama (which means "she is not pitied") and Lo-ammi (which means "not my people"). Gomer and her children were to be a visible image of the people of Israel.

In the case of Mary, she is to represent the holy Church. Like Mary the Church is both a virgin and mother. Like Mary the Church is without sin (the members are sinful, but the Church herself is without sin).
The gifts God gives to Mary are meant to be seen by God's faithful people as promises to themselves. What God has done for Mary He will do for us. Mary was made without sin; our sins are removed in baptism. Mary held the life of Jesus in her womb; we are given the life of Jesus in Holy Communion. Mary now reigns with her Son in heaven, the Bible promises us that we will one-day reign with Christ (we will examine this more fully in the last Glorious Mystery, the Coronation). Mary was taken body and soul to heaven; we will one day be brought body and soul to heaven. Mary shares in the glory of her Son, we will one-day share in Christ's glory.

Knowing that Mary represents the Church, God's great gifts to her are meant to fill us with an incredible sense of hope.

9) Who promises to bring all His faithful body and soul to heaven at the end of time.

Here is exhibit A of the previous two reflections. We see throughout the NT the promise that we will receive a glorified body at the end of time (see 1Cor 15:50-55, 2 Cor 5:1-10, and Philippians 3:21-22). In 1 Thessalonians 4:13-18 St. Paul tells us that those who are alive when Jesus comes will not have an advantage over those who have died. He says the dead will be raised and the living will be brought body and soul to meet Him.

God has given the example of the Assumption of Mary to be sign of hope of all the good things in store for His faithful people.

10) Who like all the kings in the line of David brought His Mother into His throne room. (P)

Once again, we end where we began. All the kings in the line of David had brought their mothers into the throne room to share in the glory of the Davidic king. Jesus being a king in the line of David has done the same. It would certainly be hard to understand how the God who gave us the command of "honor your father and mother" would for some reason give less honor to His Mother than all the other kings in the line of David, but that is sadly is what some Christians believe. As Catholics we believe that God in the flesh perfectly lived the commandments. We believe that He has showered glory upon His Mother. We will see the logical conclusion of this in the Last Glorious mystery, the Coronation of Mary.

Holy Mary, Mother of God, pray for us sinners
now and at the hour of our death. Amen.

Glory be to the Father,
and to the Son, and to the Holy Spirit:
As it was in the beginning,
is now, and ever shall be, world without end. Amen

Oh my Jesus, forgive our sins and save us from the power of hell.
Lead all souls into heaven especially those
most in need of your mercy. Amen

The Fifth Glorious Mystery
The Coronation of Mary

*Hail Mary, full of grace, the Lord is with you; blessed are you among women, and blessed is the fruit of your womb, **Jesus**:*

1) Who like all the kings in the line of David made His Mother Queen Mother over His Kingdom. (P)

Throughout the NT Jesus is referred to as the "son of David." We see this title used in reference to Him 17 times. Let's take a look at how the original "son of David" (Solomon) reacted the first time his mother came into his presence after he had become king. We read in 1 Kings 2:19-20:

> *Then Bathsheba went to King Solomon to speak to him for Adonijah, and the king stood up to meet her and paid her homage. Then he sat down upon his throne, and a throne was provided for the king's mother, who sat at his right. She said, "There is one small favor I would ask of you. Do not refuse me." The king said to her, "Ask it, my mother, for I will not refuse you."*

This was the beginning of what was known as "the Gebirah" (Queen Mother). As we saw in the last Mystery, every king in the line of David brought his mother into the throne room; every king made his mother the queen mother over the kingdom; every king gave his mother incredible authority; every king gave his mother a crown and a throne. In this passage we see King Solomon, although he is at this point the all-powerful king of Judah and Israel, he gets off his throne, bows before his mother and has a throne provided for her at his right hand (the hand of authority). His mother asks him for a favor and says, "do not refuse me" and Solomon responds, "ask my mother, for I will not refuse you."

We see throughout the OT that there was an office of Queen Mother. In fact, when King Asa ascended to the throne it would appear that his mother had died, but it says his grandmother was given the title of queen mother until he deposed her because of her sinfulness. In all we see five references of the term "queen mother" although as we pointed out in the last chapter, in the two Books of Kings, the name of the king's living mother was mentioned for every king in the line of David. Why did all the kings in the line of David so prominently give glory to their mother? First of course was because of the commandment to honor your father and mother. The kings in the line of David, despite their many failures, generally did a pretty good job of being faithful to this commandment.

But probably even more to the point was the kings owed their throne to their moms. How is that? Well most of the kings had many wives and many children by those wives. Polygamy was alive and well during the time of the kings of Judah. A man would most often become king because his mother was the favorite wife and she pulled strings for him to become the king. In 1 Kings 1 we see how Nathan the prophet worked with Bathsheba (Solomon's mother) to assure that Solomon would become the king. Solomon's succession to the throne was anything but guaranteed before Bathsheba acted. There is little wonder that Solomon honored her as he did. As the Bible makes clear this was the beginning of the office of queen mother. It would certainly be odd if Jesus as a king in the line of David would refuse to honor His Mother as all other kings in the line of David honored their mothers!

2) **Who made His Mother Queen of heaven and earth.**

3) **Who made His Mother Queen of angles and of men.**

4) **Who made His Mother Queen of all that is seen and unseen.**

In the OT the mother of the king was the queen mother over the entire kingdom. That is now true of the Queen Mother of Jesus. But Israel is only about 263 miles long and 71 miles at its widest and 9.3 miles at its narrowest. Roughly today Israel is about 8,000 square miles, which is not a lot of territory. The census David conducted in 2 Samuel 24 numbered 1.3 million men capable of military service, so there were probably a little over three million people in his entire kingdom. That is a far cry from the Kingdom of Jesus. Jesus' Kingdom includes all those who ever have or ever will live who will be brought to heaven. It includes the nine choirs of angels. The Kingdom of Jesus extends over the entire universe, all that is seen and unseen. And His Mother is the Queen Mother over it all. The extent that He has honored her is beyond words to describe.

5) **Who clothed His Mother with the sun.**

6) **Who put the moon under her feet.**

7) **Who gave His Mother a crown of 12 stars.**

In Revelation 12:1, Mary is described as being in heaven clothed with the glory of the heavens, *"A great sign appeared in the sky, a woman clothed with the sun, with the moon under her feet, and on her head a crown of twelve stars"* This description of Mary is obviously symbolic. After all the sun is pretty hot; she would need more than asbestos undergarments to protect her from the heat. Stars are pretty big; she'd have to have incredible neck muscles to hold up such a crown. What is the point of this description? It goes back to the book of Genesis. We are told in Genesis 1:14-19 how God created the sun, moon and stars to "govern" or "rule" the night and the day:

> *Then God said: Let there be lights in the dome of the sky, to separate day from night. Let them mark the seasons, the days and the years, and serve as lights in the dome of the sky, to illuminate the earth. And so it happened: God made the two great lights, the greater one to govern the day, and the lesser one to govern the night, and the stars. God set them in the dome of the sky, to illuminate the earth, to govern the day and the night, and to separate the light from the darkness. God saw that it was good.*

We see royal language used in the creation of the sun, moon and stars; they are to "govern" the day and the night (other translations use the word "rule"). The sun, moon and stars are supposed to remind us of the glory of God who is our true ruler. They are to be visible reminders of the place that God should have in our lives. And yet in the book of Revelation St. John describes Mary as being clothed with the sun, with the moon under her feet and on her head a crown of 12 stars. The crown of stars points us to her royalty, that she is our Queen. The sun and moon are meant to demonstrate that Mary now is clothed with the glory of God. In other words, God had shared His glory with her. She is to be sure, still a creature. But she now reigns over all creatures as the Queen Mother of the King of kings.

It is again difficult to put into the words the incredible glory that the Lord has shared with His Blessed Mother!

8) Who made His Mother a powerful intercessor for His people.

The first time we are introduced to the concept of the queen mother in the Bible she (Bathsheba) is interceding for another (1 Kings 2:19-21). Extra biblical sources indicate that the queen mothers of ancient Judah had incredible influence in the kingdom. The first miracle of Jesus is worked through the intercession of His Mother. Her intercession not only leads to the miracle of turning water into wine, but it leads to Jesus' disciples coming to believe in Him (John 2:11).

With God of course, there are no coincidences. The message of scripture and tradition points us to the fact that the Mother of Jesus is a powerful intercessor for His people.

There are of course many outside the Catholic Church who ask, "Why go to Mary when you can go right to God? That is a valid question that we will now address.

The promise of Jesus to His faithful disciples in not just they will go to heaven (which on its own is an incredible gift), but that we will reign with Jesus (see 2Timothy 2:12, Rev 5:10, 20:6, and 22:5). What does that mean? It means we will share in His royal authority. That was very different than the people living in Israel at the time of the Roman Empire were used to. The average Israeli had no illusions that he or she was reigning with Caesar. Caesar was the ruler and they were the ruled over. But there were people who shared in Caesar's authority. Pilate ruled with Caesar as did Herod. The ministers of taxation and the military and agriculture and the roads and others also shared in Caesar's authority. Well the promise of the Bible is that you and I will share in Jesus' authority.

We see this promise not only in the explicit word of "reign" but in some of the parables of the Lord. For instance, in Matthew 25:14-28 we read:

> *It will be as when a man who was going on a journey called in his servants and entrusted his possessions to them. To one he gave five talents; to another, two; to a third, one—to each according to his ability. Then he went away. Immediately the one who received five talents went and traded with them, and made another five. Likewise, the one who received two made another two. But the man who received one went off and dug a hole in the ground and buried his master's money. After a long time the master of those servants came back and settled accounts with them. The one who had received five talents came forward bringing the additional five. He said, 'Master, you gave me five talents. See, I have made five more.' His master said to him, 'Well done, my good and faithful servant. Since you were faithful in small matters, I will give you great responsibilities. Come, share your master's joy.' [Then] the one who had received two talents also came forward and said, 'Master, you gave me two talents. See, I have made two more.' His master said to him, 'Well done, my good and faithful servant. Since you were faithful in small matters, I will give you great responsibilities. Come, share your master's joy.' Then the one who had received the one talent came forward and said, 'Master, I knew you were a demanding person, harvesting where you did not plant and gathering where you did not scatter; so out of fear I went off and buried your talent in the ground. Here it is back.' His master said to him in reply, 'You wicked, lazy servant! So you knew that I harvest where I did not plant and gather where I did not scatter? Should you not then have put my money in the bank so that I could have*

got it back with interest on my return? Now then! Take the talent from him and give it to the one with ten. For to everyone who has, more will be given and he will grow rich; but from the one who has not, even what he has will be taken away. And throw this useless servant into the darkness outside, where there will be wailing and grinding of teeth.'

We see the same idea in Luke 19:11-26:

While they were listening to him speak, he proceeded to tell a parable because he was near Jerusalem and they thought that the kingdom of God would appear there immediately. So he said, "A nobleman went off to a distant country to obtain the kingship for himself and then to return. He called ten of his servants and gave them ten gold coins and told them, 'Engage in trade with these until I return.' His fellow citizens, however, despised him and sent a delegation after him to announce, 'We do not want this man to be our king.' But when he returned after obtaining the kingship, he had the servants called, to whom he had given the money, to learn what they had gained by trading. The first came forward and said, 'Sir, your gold coin has earned ten additional ones.' He replied, 'Well done, good servant! You have been faithful in this very small matter; take charge of ten cities.' Then the second came and reported, 'Your gold coin, sir, has earned five more.' And to this servant too he said, 'You, take charge of five cities.' Then the other servant came and said, 'Sir, here is your gold coin; I kept it stored away in a handkerchief, for I was afraid of you, because you are a demanding person; you take up what you did not lay down and you harvest what you did not plant.' He said to him, 'With your own words I shall condemn you, you wicked servant. You knew I was a demanding person, taking up what I

251

did not lay down and harvesting what I did not plant; why did you not put my money in a bank? Then on my return I would have collected it with interest.' And to those standing by he said, 'Take the gold coin from him and give it to the servant who has ten.' But they said to him, 'Sir, he has ten gold coins.' 'I tell you, to everyone who has, more will be given, but from the one who has not, even what he has will be taken away.

Both parables are a wonderful synopsis of the Catholic faith. In both none of the servants could have accomplished anything without what the Master gave them. This corresponds to our Catholic faith in that we can do nothing without the gifts and grace of God. Everything we have and everything we are is God's gift to us. In addition to our natural gifts the Bible makes it clear when we want to do good it is because of God's grace. When we accomplish good it is because of God's grace (Philippians 2:13). But both these parables also make it clear that we must do something with the gifts God has given. We cannot sit back and do nothing because "Jesus did it all" as some claim. No, in both these parables the ones who received the Master's gifts and did nothing with them were punished severely.

But what is most important for us to focus on here is the fact that both parables are parables of judgment. Notice that after judgment that people will share in the authority of the Master. In Matthew's gospel it says, "...I will give you great responsibilities. Come share your master's joy." In Luke we are told the one servant is to "take charge of ten cities" while the 2nd servant will "take charge of five cities." In other words, they are sharing in the royal authority of the Master. The same will be true for us in the life of heaven.

Right now, the saints reign with Christ, that is they have been put in charge of things. We have St. Joseph the patron saint of fathers; St.

John Vianney the patron saint of priests; St. Christopher the patron saint of travelers; and one of my favorites, St. Anthony who helps us when we cannot find something (if you saw my desk and house you would understand why I am so attached to Anthony). There are hundreds of patron saints that we can turn to for help.

Mary of course reigns now as Queen over all the saints and angels. If the other saints can intercede for us how much more powerful are the prayers of Mary? St. James tells us in the Bible that the prayers of the righteous person are powerful indeed (James 5:16). Who is more righteous than those who are in heaven? Who is more righteous than the Queen Mother who is clothed with the sun, the moon under her feet and on her head a crown of 12 stars?

The idea of intercessory prayer is certainly not foreign to the Bible. St. Paul recommends in 1 Timothy 2:1-3 that Christians pray for all those in authority that we might lead a tranquil life. Well if the prayers of people on earth who are still sinners can bring changes in the world, why would we hesitate to think the prayers of Mary and the other saints could effect changes in the world? Christians of all different denominations and non-denominations ask other Christians for prayers. If we ask our brothers and sisters on earth to pray for us why would we not ask or brothers and sisters in heaven to pray for us?

Some might say, "Because they are dead and they cannot hear or help us." But that is not the teaching of the Bible. The Bible teaches that the saints in heaven surround us and our very interested in our lives, so we read in Hebrews 12: 1, "*Therefore, since we are surrounded by so great a cloud of witnesses, let us rid ourselves of every burden and sin that clings to us and persevere in running the race that lies before us.*" This verse appears right after Hebrews 11 where the author speaks of the heroes of the OT. He is basically painting the picture that the saints are here cheering us on as we fight sin and strive to be faithful to the Lord. As Hebrews 12 goes on it tells us that we have not only grown close to God and Jesus, but also to "the assembly of the Firstborn enrolled in heaven" (that is our brothers and sisters on earth); we have grown close to the angels (vs 22) and to the "spirits of the just made perfect" (the saints in heaven who have been purified by the grace of purgatory). Let's take a look at Hebrews 12: 18-24:

> You have not approached that which could be touched and a blazing fire and gloomy darkness and storm and a trumpet blast and a voice speaking words such that those who heard begged that no message be further addressed to them, for they could not bear to hear the command: "If even an animal touches the mountain, it shall be stoned." Indeed, so fearful was the spectacle that Moses said, "I am terrified and trembling." No, you have approached Mount Zion and the city of the living God, the heavenly Jerusalem, and countless angels in festal gathering, and the assembly of the firstborn enrolled in heaven, and God the judge of all, and the spirits of the just made perfect, and Jesus, the mediator of a new covenant, and the sprinkled blood that speaks more eloquently than that of Abel.

This passage very powerfully reminds us that our faith is not a merely individualistic relationship between "me and Jesus." No, in faith we have grown close to the Father and the Son for sure, but also to the angels, to the Christians on earth and to the saints in heaven who have been made perfect. Those saints in heaven have also grown close to us and stand ready to intercede on our behalf, all we need to do is to turn to them for help. This is especially true of the Blessed Mother.

The question remains, "why would you go to Mary and the other saints when you can go straight to God?" The short answer is because God wants us to. Jesus came to make us a family. The family of God extends from earth to heaven. He wants us in relationship with our older brothers and sisters in the faith. He certainly wants us to be in a relationship with our Mother in heaven, the Blessed Virgin Mary. That is why Jesus gave us His Mother to be our Mother as He hung on the cross (John 19: 26-27). As Catholics we build family ties with our brothers and sisters on earth as well as those in heaven. And we of course build a relationship with our Mother in heaven who loves us as her cherished children.

9) Who sent His Mother to Guadalupe, Lourdes, Fatima, Medjugorje, and other places with messages for the people of the world.

There are of course no Bible passages that can be quoted to demonstrate that Mary has appeared in these various places. Historically, there are roughly 12 sites that the Vatican has approved as legitimate apparitions of Mary and perhaps a few dozen more that local bishops have acknowledged as genuine. Although as Catholics we are not required by faith to acknowledge any of the apparitions of Mary.

The four mentioned above are ones that have had great historical significance and are officially recognized by the universal Church. The fourth is a site that I have personally visited and witnessed a miracle.

Our Lady of Guadalupe occurred in 1531 when the Blessed Mother appeared to a peasant by the name of Juan Diego (who is now known as St. Juan Diego). The vision occurred at a place called Tepeyac in Mexico. The Blessed Mother arranged Castillian roses that were not native to Mexico on Juan Diego's tilma (or cloak) and when he brought the tilma to the local bishop there was an image of the Blessed Mother on the tilma. This apparition occurred at a time when millions of people in Europe were leaving the Catholic Church, but it led to millions coming to the faith in the Americas.

Our Lady of Lourdes appeared to a 14-year old peasant girl by the name of Bernadette Soubirous in Lourdes, France in 1858. Mary revealed herself to the peasant girl (now known as St. Bernadette) as "the Immaculate Conception." She told Bernadette to start digging and a stream appeared. That stream continues to this day and there have been more than 60 verified healing miracles that have taken place in the waters of Lourdes.

Our Lady of Fatima occurred when Our Lady appeared to three peasant children, Lucia Santos and her two cousins Jacinta and Francisco Marto in 1917 in Fatima, Portugal. The government of Portugal at the time was very anti-Catholic and the apparitions brought persecutions to the children and their families. Mary told the children there would be a great miracle on October 13th of that year. Thousands of people flocked to Fatima to see the miracle and were not disappointed. The crowd that was estimated at between 30,000 and 100,000 people reported the miracle of the sun. Below are the descriptions of various people as recorded in the on-line encyclopedia Wikipedia:

> *"The incessant rain had ceased and there was a thin layer of cloud. Lúcia, seeing light rising from the lady's hands and the sun appearing as a silver disk, called out "look at the sun". She later had no memory of saying this. Witnesses later spoke of the sun appearing to change colors and rotate like a wheel. Witnesses gave widely varying descriptions of the "sun's*

dance". Poet Afonso Lopes Vieira and schoolteacher Delfina Lopes (with her students and other witnesses in the town of Alburita), reported that the solar phenomenon was visible up to forty kilometers away.

Columnist Avelino de Almeida of O Seculo (Portugal's most influential newspaper, which was pro-government in policy and avowedly anti-clerical) reported the following: "Before the astonished eyes of the crowd, whose aspect was biblical as they stood bare-headed, eagerly searching the sky, the sun trembled, made sudden incredible movements outside all cosmic laws - the sun 'danced' according to the typical expression of the people." Eye specialist Dr. Domingos Pinto Coelho, writing for the newspaper Ordem reported "The sun, at one moment surrounded with scarlet flame, at another aureoled in yellow and deep purple, seemed to be in an exceeding fast and whirling movement, at times appearing to be loosened from the sky and to be approaching the earth, strongly radiating heat". The special reporter for the October 17, 1917 edition of the Lisbon daily, O Dia, reported the following, "...the silver sun, enveloped in the same gauzy purple light was seen to whirl and turn in the circle of broken clouds...The light turned a beautiful blue, as if it had come through the stained-glass windows of a cathedral, and spread itself over the people who knelt with outstretched hands...people wept and prayed with uncovered heads, in the presence of a miracle they had awaited. The seconds seemed like hours, so vivid were they."

Tens of thousands of people saw the sun dance including many who were anti-Catholic and anti-religion. It would certainly seem like God is trying to get our attention through the Blessed Mother.

And finally, the apparition occurring in Medjugorje, Croatia. These apparitions have been occurring for over 30 years. I made a pilgrimage there and was there on the 15th anniversary of the start of the apparitions. One evening as I and one of my parishioners were coming down from the mount of apparition we came around a corner and there were a group of people looking in the direction of the sun. They were saying things like, "Isn't that amazing," and "I've never seen anything like this before." I looked in the direction they were looking and saw the sun spinning in one direction and then the other. The sun pulsated and changed colors. The parishioner I was with also looked at the sun with amazement.

I wondered why I was blessed to see what I did. I have often thought that God gives visible manifestations to people who have weak faith in order to strengthen them. Was God telling me my faith was weak? I really do not understand what I saw or why I saw it, but I did. It would be prudent to ask, "Do these apparitions fit in with biblical patterns?" The answer is an absolute yes. We see throughout scripture that God often sent those closest to Him, the holy angles to bring messages to the people of the world. These angelic apparitions occurred in both the OT and NT. But with the Incarnation and saving work of the Lord it is clear that the one closest to God now is the Blessed Mother. She has been called "the chosen of the Father," "the Mother of the eternal Son," and "the spouse of the Holy Spirit." It would be totally in keeping with the biblical pattern of God to send Mary to the earth with messages for the people of the world.

The common theme of most of the apparitions in the last century is prayer and repentance. In Fatima, the Blessed Mother gave the children a glimpse of hell. They were so terrified that they spent much of the rest of their lives doing works of fasting and penance on behalf

258

of "poor sinners" in the hopes of saving some of them. It would certainly appear that God is trying to get the attention of the human race as we see all of these apparitions of Our Lady. It would certainly be wise for all of us to seek repentance of our sins and to devote ourselves to prayerful reflection on the revealed truths of our faith.

As Mary's intercession led to the disciples coming to believe in Him at the wedding feast of Cana, Mary's intervention has led to millions coming to the faith (as in the case of Guadalupe) and others being renewed in faith. Mary's greatest desire is to lead others to know, love and serve her Son. She says to us today as she said to the servants at the wedding feast of Cana, "Do whatever He tells you to do."

10) Who like all kings in the line of David made His Mother the Queen Mother over His Kingdom. (P)

If I were ever to make a movie of the rosary I would begin it with portraying Mary in great glory surrounded by all the angels and saints who look at her with love and devotion. Our Lady would be saying something like, "Look what my Son has done for me. Whoever would have thought that a little peasant girl from an insignificant town in an insignificant country could ever experience such glory. I owe it all to my loving Son. He has showered glory on me and He wants you to share in His glory as well. Let me tell you the story." With that the scene would switch to Nazareth when Mary was a young girl with the angel appearing to her.

The Jewish people at the time of our Lord expected a messiah that would reestablish the kingdom of David. They of course would have anticipated that the Messiah would heap glory upon His Mother as all the other kings in the line of David had upon their mothers. Our belief in the Queenship of Mary merely makes us Catholics "Bible

259

Christians" because what Jesus has done in sharing His glory with His Mother is totally consistent with the practice of every Davidic king in the Bible. It is certainly inconceivable that there are many who identify themselves as "Bible Christians" who are antagonistic to this biblical theme of the Queen Mother. We need to know and understand that the Queen of heaven and earth loves us and is there to help us grow in faith and love!

Holy Mary, Mother of God, pray for us sinners
now and at the hour of our death. Amen.
Glory be to the Father,
and to the Son, and to the Holy Spirit:

As it was in the beginning,
is now, and ever shall be, world without end. Amen

Oh my Jesus, forgive our sins and save us from the power of hell.
Lead all souls into heaven especially those
most in need of your mercy. Amen

Epilogue

We finish this book with the understanding that like all the kings in David's line, Jesus has given His Mother a glorious role in His Kingdom. Like Bathsheba the mother of Solomon, Jesus has given His Mother a throne at His right hand. He has made her a powerful intercessor for His people. He in His love for us has given us His Mother to be our Mother. As Eve became the "mother of all the living" Mary has now become the "Mother of all those born again in Christ."

God's plan of salvation is a family plan. Jesus came to conquer the effects of sin in the world. In Genesis we are told how sin separated us from God and from one another. Jesus came to unite us to God and each other. He came to make us a family, His family, a community of love. Why is this important to the Lord? Because we are made in the image and likeness of God who has revealed Himself to us as a community of love. God is not a solitary figure, but is rather Father, Son and Holy Spirit. We cannot be fully human outside of community.

The rugged individualism that is rampant in our nation is not consistent with our deepest nature and desires. In creating us God made it so that we are to be born into a community of love that we call the family. In His plan a man and woman are made one in the sacrament of marriage. They are meant to be united in love and as they express their love for one another and new life is created. Each one of us is meant to be love come-to-life. Children are meant to be nurtured in this environment of love between a husband and a wife. The human family in their love for one another is meant to be a living icon of the all-powerful God who is love.

In saving us we see the same pattern. Jesus is the Bridegroom and His bride is the Church. As Jesus expresses His love for His bride we are "born again" into His family. The baptismal font is the womb of "Holy Mother the Church." As our natural mothers feed us, clothe us, clean us, and care for us when we are hurt; our spiritual mother the Church feeds us with the finest food and drink (the Holy Eucharist), clothes us with virtue through Her wise teaching, washes us clean in reconciliation when we have fallen into sin, and cares for us in our infirmities through the sacrament of the sick.

Unfortunately, many today reject the Wisdom of God that comes to us through the bride of Christ. Mark Twain once stated how when he was 14 he thought his old man was a fool; when he was 21 he was amazed at how smart his father got in just seven years. Many of the children of the Church are like 14-year-old Mark Twain (actually Samuel Clemens) who scoff at the Church as ignorant and behind the times. As many of the children of the Church ignore Her we see more and more dysfunction, more and more heartache, more and more exploitation. Many today wander, lost in a moral wilderness because in our arrogance we believe that Jesus failed to keep His promise to guide the Church and feel free to ignore the bride of Christ.

I know when I was a child if I was in any way disrespectful to my mom, dad would go ballistic. I will not share any of those stories, but suffice it to say it was never a wise option in our home to ignore mom. Well Jesus does not love His bride less than my dad loved his. Right now, we are an adolescent culture in rebellion against the Lord and His bride. In our so-called sophistication we have turned our backs on the font of truth and wisdom. Mark Twain opened his eyes to the wisdom of his dad, as a people we would do well to recognize the wisdom of our Mother the Church.

One of the great mysteries of life is the fact that God made us so imperfect. He could have made us with perfect knowledge of mathematics, engineering, medicine and common sense. But He did not! Why? Because He wants us to know that we need one another. It is often because of our weaknesses that we turn to others and bond with them. If we were perfect in every way we would have no need for others.

In the same way in saving us God has made us dependent on others. We cannot baptize ourselves, we need someone from the community to do that for us. We cannot forgive ourselves, we need to humbly confess to a minister of the Church to receive God's forgiveness. No one can ordain themselves a priest, a man needs to turn to the bishop for that. On a natural level we are a bundle of needs who could not survive without the community. On a spiritual level it is the same. God has made us a bundle of needs that requires us to turn to the community if we are to survive and thrive. In receiving from the community and then in turn giving of ourselves to build the community we better represent God in the world who is a community of love.

In God of course there are no needs, but with God there is one Will. The Father never argues with the Son. There is perfect love, perfect self-giving, perfect harmony. On the human level we each have our own wills and that brings many clashes. If we were totally self-sufficient that would most likely lead to our being isolated little islands unto ourselves. God in His love made us needy so that we can realize how dependent we are on others.

In our salvation St. Paul teaches us that we need one another. He teaches in 1 Corinthians 12:12-21:

As a body is one though it has many parts, and all the parts of the body, though many, are one body, so also Christ. For in one Spirit we were all baptized into one body, whether Jews or Greeks, slaves or free persons, and we were all given to drink of one Spirit.

Now the body is not a single part, but many. If a foot should say, "Because I am not a hand I do not belong to the body," it does not for this reason belong any less to the body. Or if an ear should say, "Because I am not an eye I do not belong to the body," it does not for this reason belong any less to the body. If the whole body were an eye, where would the hearing be? If the whole body were hearing, where would the sense of smell be? But as it is, God placed the parts, each one of them, in the body as he intended. If they were all one part, where would the body be? But as it is, there are many parts, yet one body. The eye cannot say to the hand, "I do not need you," nor again the head to the feet, "I do not need you."

The Bible makes it clear we need each other in the journey of salvation. No member of the Body of Christ can say to any other member, "I don't need you." And yet many today believe they do not need the Church. And still more believe they do not need Mary and the saints. But any way you look at it, clearly those attitudes are very much contrary to the teaching of the Bible. We need each other, we need the Church, and we need Mary and the other saints.

Jesus gave us His Mother as He hung on the cross to be our Mother. Mary's greatest desire is to bring us closer to Her Son, our Lord, Jesus Christ. The rosary is one way where our Mother can take us by the hand and help us enter more fully into the mysteries of the faith. Please allow your Mother in heaven to lead you to her Son.

What you have found in this book is just one man's method of praying the rosary that has enriched his life. This did not come down from on high. This is not the revealed wisdom of some great spiritual guru which you need to follow to the letter. This is just one sinful man's reflections on some of the great mysteries of faith. If you find this helpful to your spiritual life that is wonderful. If you disagree with the reflections that I have designated as primary that is certainly acceptable. Please use what you find helpful and disregard whatever you find distracting (I am speaking here on the methodology, not the revealed truth of the mysteries).

Pray well, pray often and may our good and gracious Mother lead you to a deeper love of Her all-powerful Son.

Mystery Summaries

Joyful Mysteries

Preliminary beads—Faith---Hope---Love

Annunciation

1. **Who chose Mary from all eternity to be His Mother.**
2. Who sent the angel Gabriel to ask Mary to consent to be His Mother.
3. Whose Mother heard the angel say, "Hail full of Grace."
4. Whose Mother was frightened by the angel and wondered what the greeting meant.
5. Whose Mother heard the angel say, "Do not be afraid Mary, for you have found favor with God."
6. Whose mother heard the angel say, "you are to conceive a Son and name Him Jesus and He will ascend to the throne of His father David.
7. Whose Mother said to the angel, "How can this be since I do not know man?"
8. Whose Mother heard the angel say, "The Holy Spirit will overshadow you, hence the child to be born will be called the Son of the Most High."
9. Whose Mother heard the angel say, "Elizabeth your relative has also conceived a son in her old age, and this is the sixth month for her who was called barren; for nothing will be impossible to God."
10. **Whose Mother said, "I am the handmaid of the Lord, may it be done to me according to your word."**

Visitation

1. **Who made His Mother the new Ark of the Covenant.**
2. Whose Mother made haste to the hill country.
3. Whose Mother heard Elizabeth say, "Who am I that the Mother of my Lord should come to me?"
4. Whose Mother heard Elizabeth say, "The moment your greeting reached my ears the baby leapt with joy in my womb."
5. Whose Mother heard Elizabeth say, "Blessed are you who believed that what was spoken to you by the Lord would be fulfilled."
6. Whose Mother said, "My soul proclaims the greatness of the Lord…"
7. Whose Mother said, "…. my spirit rejoices in God my Savior."
8. Whose Mother said, "God has cast down the mighty from their thrones and lifted up the lowly."
9. Whose Mother stayed with Elizabeth for three months and then returned home.
10. **Who made His Mother the new Ark of the Covenant.**

Birth of the Savior

1. **Who was born in the city of David.**
2. **Who was born in Bethlehem, which means "house of bread."**
3. **Who was placed in a feeding trough after His birth.**
4. Whose parents made a difficult journey to Bethlehem when Mary was nine months pregnant.
5. Whose parents found no room in the Inn when they arrived in Bethlehem.
6. Who was born in a stable.
7. Who was held with such great love in His Mother's arms.
8. Who was sung of by angels and adored by simple shepherds and great Magi.
9. Whose birth was a threat to the lifestyle of King Herod.
10. **Who was born in the City of David/ the house of bread.**

The Presentation in the Temple

1. **Whose parents faithfully obeyed the laws of the Lord.**
2. Whose parents had Him circumcised on the 8th day as the Law of the Lord required.
3. Whose parents presented Him in the Temple on the 40th day as the law of the Lord required.
4. Who was recognized by Anna who prayed day and night in the Temple.
5. Whose parents heard Simeon say, "Now Master you can let your servant go in peace...."
6. Whose parents heard Simeon say, "...for my eyes have seen your salvation..."
7. Whose parents heard Simeon say that their Son was the light to the nations and the glory of Israel.
8. Whose parents heard Simeon say that their Son would be the rise and the fall of many in Israel.
9. Whose Mother heard Simeon say that her soul would be pierced with the sword of sorrow so that the hearts of many would be laid bare.
10. **Whose parents faithfully obeyed the laws of the Lord.**

The Finding of the Child Jesus in the Temple

1. **Whose parent made great sacrifices for the practice of their faith.**
2. Whose parents brought Jesus to Jerusalem for Passover when He was twelve; as was their custom.
3. Who was filled with zeal for His Father's house.
4. Whose parents searched frantically for Him for three days.
5. Who amazed all those in the Temple with the Wisdom of His questions and answers.
6. Who heard His Mother say, "Son, why have you done this to us? Your father and I have been searching for you with great anxiety."
7. Who said to His Mother, "Why were you searching for me? Did you not know that I must be in my Father's house?"
8. Who returned to Nazareth with Joseph and Mary and was obedient to them. (Luke 2:51)
9. Whose Mother pondered all these things in her heart.
10. **Whose parents made great sacrifices for the practice of their faith.**

Luminous Mysteries

Preliminary beads—Faith---Hope---Love

The Baptism of the Lord

1. **Who first revealed the Trinity on the day of His baptism.**
2. **Who chose to become the "Christ" through the ministry of the Levite, John the Baptist.**
3. Who heard John the Baptist say, "Behold the Lamb of God…"
4. Who heard John the Baptist say, "… the Lamb who takes away the sins of the world."
5. Who heard John the Baptist say, "You should be baptizing me, I should not be baptizing you."
6. Who said to John, "We must do this to fulfill all righteousness."
7. Who would later teach, "Amen, amen, I say to you, no one can enter the Kingdom of God without being born of water and Spirit."
8. Who was anointed by the Holy Spirit in the form of a dove.
9. Who heard the voice of the Father say, "This is my beloved Son in whom I am well pleased."
10. **Who first revealed the Trinity on the day of His Baptism.**

The Wedding Feast of Cana

1. **Who chose to first manifest His glory through the intercession of Mary.**
2. Who chose to first manifest His glory at a wedding banquet.
3. Whose mother Mary was invited to a wedding feast in Cana of Galilee; Jesus and His disciples were also invited.
4. Who heard His Mother say, "They have no wine."
5. Who said to His Mother, "Woman, what's this between you and me?"
6. Who said to His Mother, "My hour has not yet come."
7. Whose Mother said to the servants, "Do whatever He tells you to do."
8. Who presented the finest wine after a lesser had been served.
9. Whose disciples began to believe in Him after the miracle.
10. **Whose Mother believed in Him before the miracle; it was her faith that led to the miracle.**

The Preaching of the Kingdom

1. **Whose first sermon was, "Repent for the Kingdom of God is at hand."**
2. **Who taught that the Kingdom of Heaven is manifested on earth through His holy Church.**
3. Who said the Kingdom is like a man who planted good seed, but an enemy comes and plants weeds.
4. Who taught that the Kingdom of God is like a fisherman who caught all kinds of fish, good as well as bad.
5. Who said the Kingdom of heaven is like a merchant in search of fine pearls. When he finds the pearl of great price he sells everything else and buys that one pearl.
6. Who taught that the Kingdom is like a king who threw a wedding banquet for his son .
7. Who taught that in the Kingdom of God our receiving of forgiveness is related to our giving of forgiveness.

8. Who said to Simon, son of Jonah, "You are rock and on this rock I will build my church."
9. Who said to Simon Peter, "I will give you the keys of the kingdom of heaven. Whatever you bind on earth, I will hold bound in heaven. Whatever you loose on earth, shall be loosed in heaven."
10. **Who taught that the Kingdom of Heaven is manifested on earth through His holy Church.**

The Transfiguration

1. **Who wanted to demonstrate that the law and the prophets were pointing to Him and were fulfilled by Him.**
2. Who wanted to give the Apostles a glimpse of His glory before He entered into His Passion.
3. Who took Peter, James and John to a high mountain to pray with them.
4. Whose clothes became dazzling white; whiter than is humanly possible.
5. Whose face radiated the very glory of God.
6. Who appeared with Moses, the giver of the law.
7. Who appeared with Elijah, the greatest of the prophets.
8. Who spoke to Moses and Elijah about His upcoming exodus that was to take place in Jerusalem.
9. Who said to the Apostles, "Tell no one of the vision until the Son of Man has risen from the dead."
10. **Who wanted to demonstrate that the law and the prophets were pointing to Him and fulfilled by Him.**

The Last Supper

1. **Who gave us His own Body and Blood at the Last Supper.**
2. Who said to the Apostles that He earnestly desired to eat this Passover with them.
3. Who ordained the Apostles priests of the new covenant through the prayers and the washing of the feet.
4. Who prayed that His disciples would be one as He and the Father are one.
5. Who prayed that there be such perfect unity among His disciples that the world would come to believe in Him.
6. Who took bread, blessed it, broke it and gave it to His disciples saying, "take this all of you and eat it, for this is my body."
7. Who took the Chalice filled with wine and said, "This is my blood."
8. Who said to the Apostles, "This is the blood of the new and eternal covenant, which will be poured out for you and for many for the forgiveness of sin."
9. Who commanded the Apostles to "Do this in remembrance of me."
10. **Who gave us His own Body and Blood at the Last Supper.**

The Sorrowful Mysteries

Preliminary Beads—Faith—Hope---Love

The Agony in the Garden

1. **Who agonized over my sins.**
2. Who after singing the "great hallel" went to a garden to be tempted.
3. Who said to the Apostles, "Watch and pray that you may not be put to the test."
4. Who prayed, "Father if you are willing, take this cup away from me...."
5. Who prayed, "... not my will, but yours be done."
6. Who sweat blood over my sins.
7. Who said to the Apostles, "Could you not watch one hour?"
8. Who said to the Apostles, "...the spirit is willing, but the flesh is weak."
9. Who was betrayed by the kiss of a friend.
10. **Who agonized over the sins of the world.**

The Scourging at the Pillar

1. **Who suffered an agonizing scourging for my sins.**
2. Who was found guilty of blasphemy by the Sanhedrin.
3. Who was brought before Pilate, then Herod and back to Pilate for judgment.
4. Who said to Pilate, "For this I was born. For this I came into the world, to testify to the truth. Everyone who belongs to the truth hears my voice."
5. Who received 39 lashes with the whip.
6. Who was scourged with a whip that had three cords.
7. Who was scourged with a whip that had bone and metal imbedded that was designed to rip the flesh.
8. Whose scourging fulfilled scripture.
9. Whose scourging shows man's inhumanity to man.
10. **Who suffered an agonizing scourging for the redemption of the world.**

The Crowning with Thorns

1. **God's eternal truth who was mocked.**
2. Who had a crown of thorns placed on His sacred head, fulfilling scripture.
3. Who had a robe of royal purple placed over His shoulders.
4. Before whom the guards fell on their knees, mockingly saying, "Hail, King of the Jews."
5. Who is the King of the Jews.
6. Who is the King of Kings.
7. Who heard Pilate say to the crowd, 'Behold the man."
8. Who heard the crowd yell, "Crucify Him. Crucify Him."
9. Who heard the high priest say, "We have no king but Caesar."
10. **God's eternal truth who was mocked.**

Jesus Carries His Cross

1. **Who carried the cross for my salvation.**
2. **Who was to be nailed to a tree because our first parents sinned at a tree.**
3. Who was given the cross because Pilate washed his hands of His (Jesus') fate.
4. Who fell again and again and again under the weight of my sin.
5. Who met His Blessed Mother along the way.
6. Who was helped to carry His cross by Simon.
7. Whose bloody faced was wiped by Veronica.
8. Who said to the women of Jerusalem, "Don't weep for me, but for yourselves and your children."
9. Who was stripped of His clothing.
10. **Who carried His cross for the salvation of the world.**

The Crucifixion

1. **Who was crucified for my salvation.**
2. Who was nailed to the cross so that I might be forgiven.
3. Who prayed, "Father forgive them for they know not what they do."
4. Who said to His Mother, "Woman, behold your son."
5. Who said to the beloved disciple, "behold your Mother."
6. Who said to the good thief, "today you will be with Me in paradise."
7. Who prayed, "My God, My God, why have you forsaken Me."
8. Who prayed, "It is Finished."
9. The new Adam whose side was opened and water, symbolizing baptism; and blood, symbolizing the Holy Eucharist, flowed from the Temple of His body, forming His Bride.
10. **Whose Mother held the lifeless Body of her Son in her arms.**

The Glorious Mysteries

Preliminary Beads—Faith—Hope---Love

The Resurrection

1. **Who conquered sin and death on the day of the Resurrection.**
2. Who rose from the dead on the third day in fulfillment of scripture.
3. Who rose from the dead on the 8th day; Sunday, the first day of the week to demonstrate that there is a new creation.
4. Who appeared to Mary Magdalene on the day of the Resurrection.
5. Who appeared to His Blessed Mother in a garden.
6. Who opened the scriptures to the disciples on the road to Emmaus.
7. Whose disciples recognized Him in the "breaking of the bread."
8. Who said to the Apostles "peace be with you."
9. Who breathed on the Apostles saying, "Receive the Holy Spirit, whose sins you forgive are forgiven them, whose sins you retain are retained."
10. **The Good Shepherd who entrusted the shepherd's staff to Peter.**

The Ascension into Heaven

1. **Who ascended into heaven to prepare a place for me.**
2. Whose last instructions to the Apostles was to go out and teach all nations.
3. Whose last instructions to His Apostles was to baptize all nations in the name of the Father, the Son, and the Holy Spirit.
4. Who took His place at the right hand of the Father.
5. Who took His place as the Lord of lords and King of kings.
6. God in the flesh who was adored by the angels.
7. Who trusted Peter who denied Him to be the leader of His Church.
8. Who trusted the Apostles who abandoned Him to carry on His saving work.
9. Who trusts me, though a sinner, to be His instrument in the world today.
10. **Who ascended into heaven to prepare a place for His faithful people.**

The Descent of the Holy Spirit

1. **Who promised to send His Holy Spirit to guide us in all truth.**
2. Whose Apostles prayed for nine days for the coming of the Spirit.
3. Whose Apostles were praying with Mary when the Holy Spirit came upon them.
4. Who sent the Holy Spirit in the form of a mighty wind.
5. Who sent the Holy Spirit in the form of tongues of fire.
6. Whose Holy Spirit filled the Apostles with courage and other gifts.
7. Whose Apostles won 3,000 converts on the day of Pentecost.
8. Who sends the Holy Spirit to change bread and wine into His holy Body and Precious Blood.
9. Who sends the Holy Spirit so that all the sacraments will be efficacious.
10. **Who promised to send the Holy Spirit so that we can know the truth.**

The Assumption of Mary

1. **Who like all the kings in the line of David brought His Mother into His throne room.**
2. Who prepared a special place for His Mother.
3. Who brought His Mother body and soul to heaven at the end of her earthly life.
4. Who prefigured Mary's Assumption in the life of Enoch.
5. Who prefigured Mary's Assumption in the life of Elijah.
6. Who prefigured the Assumption of Mary in the life of Moses.
7. Who made His Mother a sign of hope for all His faithful.
8. Who wills His faithful to see His gifts to Mary as promises to themselves.
9. Who promises to bring all His faithful body and soul to heaven at the end of time.
10. **Who like all the kings in the line of David brought His Mother into His throne room.**

The Coronation of Mary

1. **Who like all the kings in the line of David made His Mother Queen Mother over His Kingdom.**
2. Who made His Mother Queen of heaven and earth.
3. Who made His Mother Queen of angles and of men.
4. Who made His Mother Queen of all that is seen and unseen.
5. Who clothed His Mother with the sun.
6. Who put the moon under her feet.
7. Who gave His Mother a crown of 12 stars.
8. Who made His Mother a powerful intercessor for His people.
9. Who sent His Mother to Guadalupe, Lourdes, Fatima, Medjugorje, and other places with messages for the people of the world.
10. **Who like all kings in the line of David made His Mother the Queen Mother over His Kingdom.**

273

Made in the USA
Columbia, SC
24 April 2018